# LOST SPRINGFIELD

## MASSACHUSETTS

# LOST SPRINGFIELD

## MASSACHUSETTS

DEREK STRAHAN

THE History PRESS

Published by The History Press
Charleston, SC
www.historypress.net



First published 2017

Manufactured in the United States

ISBN 9781467136662

Library of Congress Control Number: 2016953504

# CONTENTS

CONTENTS

# ACKNOWLEDGEMENTS

Writing this book has required a considerable amount of research from books, newspapers and primary sources in order to gather information. The *Springfield Republican Historical Archive* has been particularly valuable in uncovering long-lost details about people and places in Springfield's history. Other helpful resources have included *Springfield— 350 Years: A Pictorial History* by Donald J. D'Amato; *Springfield, 1636–1986*, edited by Michael F. Konig and Martin Kaufman; and *Town into City: Springfield, Massachusetts, and the Meaning of Community, 1840–1880* by Michael H. Frisch.

Many of the photographs in this book came from the Library of Congress, in particular their collection of early twentieth-century glass plate negatives from the Detroit Publishing Company. Other photographs were provided by Stephen Davis of the Springfield Preservation Trust and Jeffrey Monseau, the College Archivist at Springfield College.

I would also like to thank Edward Mack, my editor at The History Press, for his guidance and support; my parents, David and Debora, who helped instill in me an appreciation for history and a love for writing; and my wife, Melissa, for all of her encouragement throughout the writing process.

# INTRODUCTION

At the start of the twentieth century, Springfield was a prosperous, rapidly growing city. Founded in 1636, it was the oldest settlement in western Massachusetts, but for many years, its growth had stagnated. Hampered by poor farmland, its original boundaries shrank in the 1700s, as agricultural communities like Longmeadow, West Springfield and Wilbraham broke away and formed new towns. By the first census in 1790, its borders covered just present-day Springfield and Chicopee, with only 1,574 people living here.

This trend began to change with the Industrial Revolution, though. With plenty of cheap, mostly uninhabited land, Springfield was an ideal location for industries such as the Springfield Armory, which was established in 1794. By the 1840s, railroad development made Springfield a major transportation crossroads, spurring further industrial and commercial growth. With over twelve thousand residents, it was incorporated as a city in 1852.

Springfield's growing prosperity drew entrepreneurs and inventors, who established successful businesses here. These businesses, in turn, brought workers, both immigrants as well as residents of the surrounding farming towns. Land that had been considered barren for farming purposes was instead developed into residential neighborhoods, turning Springfield into the "City of Homes."

By 1900, Springfield had a population of over sixty-two thousand, and it had become the economic and cultural center of western Massachusetts. It had a thriving commercial center along Main Street and factories that

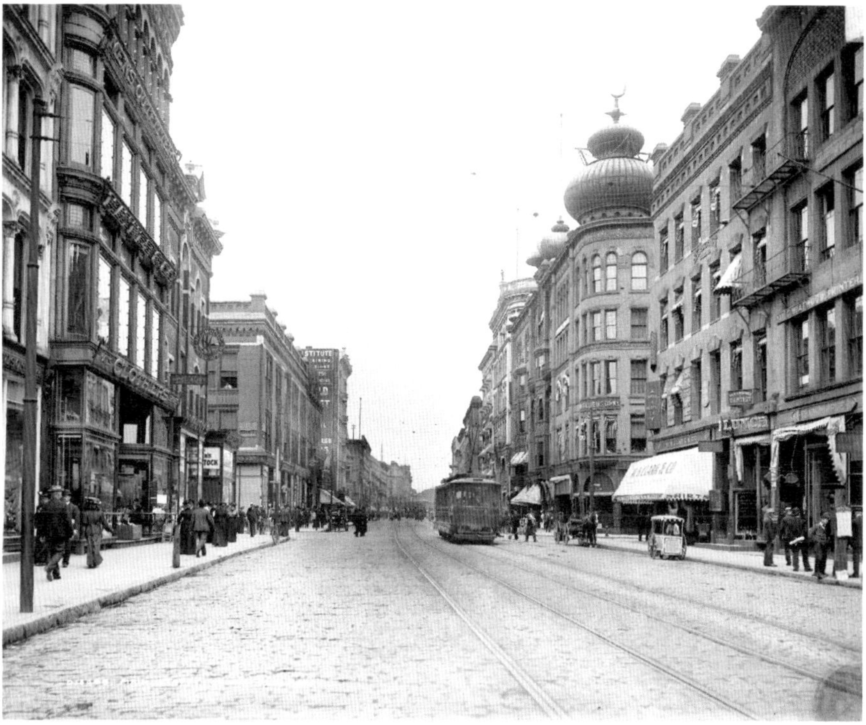

The view looking north on Main Street from Hillman Street, around 1905. *Library of Congress.*

employed thousands of people, manufacturing a variety of goods that were sold around the world. Downtown Springfield was the hub of the region's transportation, which included a network of electric trolleys that connected the city's neighborhoods and its suburbs. The city also offered residents many educational opportunities, including modern school buildings, a public library and several museums, and in the people's leisure time, they could enjoy the growing public park system, which included as its centerpiece the recently opened Forest Park.

This prosperity continued for several more decades, but by the mid-twentieth century, Springfield was in decline. Many of its businesses closed during the Great Depression, and in the years that followed, others closed or relocated outside the city, culminating with the closure of the Springfield Armory in 1968. As was the case in most other American cities at the time, residents began to leave the city, too. The 1940 census was the first in 150 years to show a drop in Springfield's population, with the automobile making it easier for middle-class families to live in the suburbs and commute to work in the city.

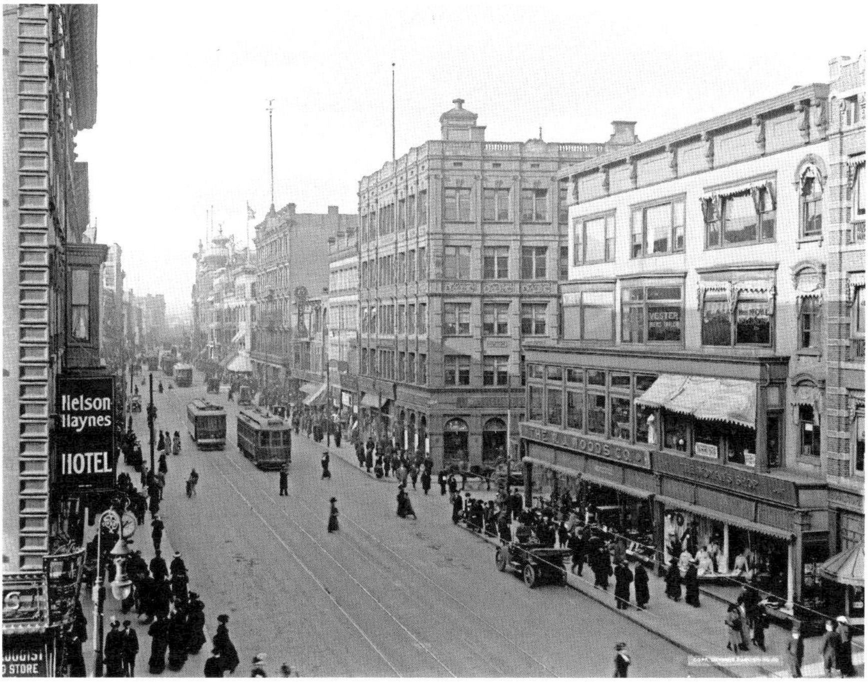


Looking north on Main Street near the corner of Harrison Avenue, around 1910–15. Nearly all the buildings on the right have since been demolished. *Library of Congress.*

Despite all of these changes, the prosperity of the late nineteenth and early twentieth centuries has left its mark on Springfield. The armory still stands on the hill overlooking downtown Springfield, and many of the other historic factory buildings in the city have been converted into apartments. Main Street is still lined with commercial buildings dating as far back as the mid-nineteenth century, and downtown Springfield has a wide variety of historic and architecturally significant churches and public buildings. Many historic homes are still standing, from Gilded Age mansions on Maple Street to Victorian town houses on Mattoon Street and the hundreds of Queen Anne houses in the McKnight neighborhood.

However, along with all of the historic buildings that have been preserved in Springfield, many others have been lost over the years. Some were destroyed by fire, and others were demolished to build better replacements. Some were demolished for large-scale urban renewal or highway construction projects, and others were taken down for promising plans that never materialized. For some, their demise was met with public outcry, but many others were lost during a time when their historical significance was either unknown or

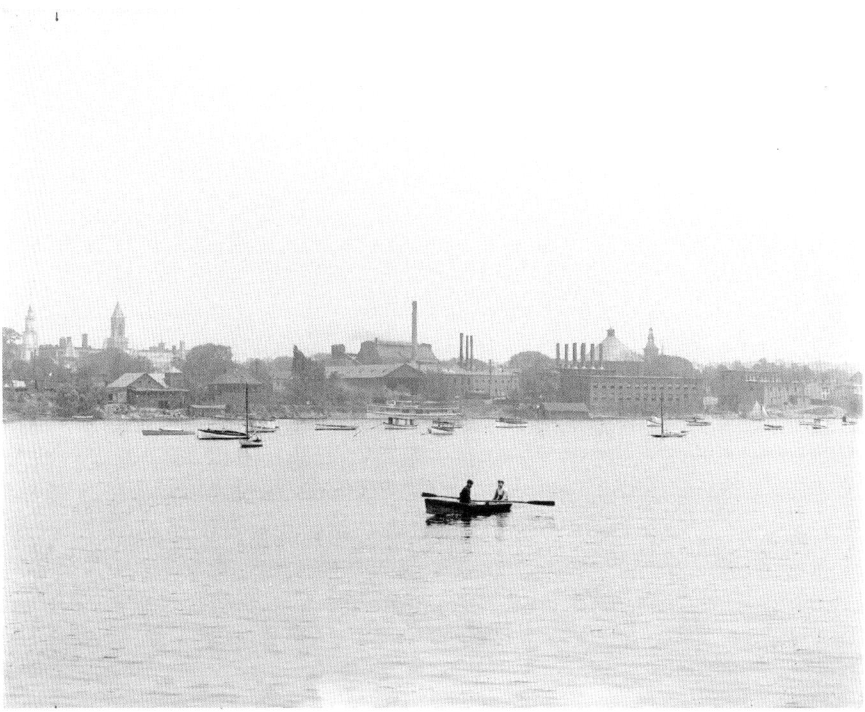

Springfield from the Connecticut River, around 1900–10, long before Interstate 91 was built along the riverfront. *Library of Congress.*

underappreciated. Regardless, though, each of these buildings contributed something to the history of the city, through the people who lived and worked in them and the important events that took place in them, sometimes shaping not just the city but also the entire country and the rest of the world.

1

# CHURCHES

As was the case in any Puritan town of the time, one of the first priorities of Springfield's early settlers was to establish a church. The following year, George Moxon became the first pastor of what would become the First Church of Christ. This Congregational church was not just the first; it was the only church in Springfield throughout the seventeenth and eighteenth centuries.

This began to change in the early 1800s, when theological dissention within Congregational churches across New England led to the formation of the Unitarian church in Springfield, the Church of the Unity. At the same time, Springfield's growth brought new residents and a greater diversity of believers, including Methodists, Baptists and Episcopalians.

By the late 1800s, there were at least thirty-two religious organizations in Springfield, representing everything from Catholicism to Swedenborgianism. Many of these historic church buildings are still standing, such as St. Michael's Cathedral on State Street, North Congregational Church on Salem Street, Memorial Church in the North End and Christ Church Cathedral on Chestnut Street. However, Springfield has also seen a number of historically significant church buildings demolished over the years.

## FIRST CHURCH

The oldest existing church building in Springfield is Old First Church, built in 1819. It was preceded, though, by three earlier meetinghouses of the colonial era, all of which were located on or around the present-day Court Square.

The first was built in 1645, at the southeast corner of Court Square, with the main entrance facing south toward what is now Elm Street. It measured forty feet by twenty-five feet and had two turrets, one of which was for the bell while the other was used as a "watch-howse." At the time, there was little currency in the colonies, so instead of a tax, everyone was required to contribute twenty-eight days of work. The town also hired carpenter Thomas Cooper for the project, who was paid eighty pounds sterling worth of "wheate, pease, pork, wampum, debts and labor" for his efforts.

Cooper was killed twenty years later when the Agawam Indians raided Springfield during King Philip's War. Three others were killed, and twenty-five houses and thirty-five barns were burned; however, the church survived the attack. By then, though, it was too small for the growing community. A year before the attack, the town voted to build a new one, citing "want of roome in the Meeting house for Our Peoples convenient attending on the Publike worship of God," but the war delayed its construction until 1677.

There are no surviving illustrations of the second meetinghouse, but it would not have looked like the traditional New England church design, which did not become commonplace until the early 1700s. It was much more expensive than the first meetinghouse, costing the town £400. The expense ledger for the construction shows that some were still paid with in-kind goods, such as two quarts of "drinke" for the person who made the window glass and a quart of rum for the "hands to raise the Ladder."

This second meetinghouse remained in use for the next seventy-five years, and during this time, it was the center of a notable controversy within the church. After the death of longtime pastor Daniel Brewer in 1733, the congregation chose Robert Breck, a young Harvard graduate, as a candidate. However, several Connecticut pastors, including future Yale president Thomas Clap, had heard him preach before and warned Springfield that he held theologically unorthodox views. The other clerics also accused him of stealing books during his time at Harvard.

The other pastors in Hampshire County, including Jonathan Edwards of Northampton, met in Springfield to examine Breck's beliefs and advised the Springfield church against selecting Breck. However, he was popular with the

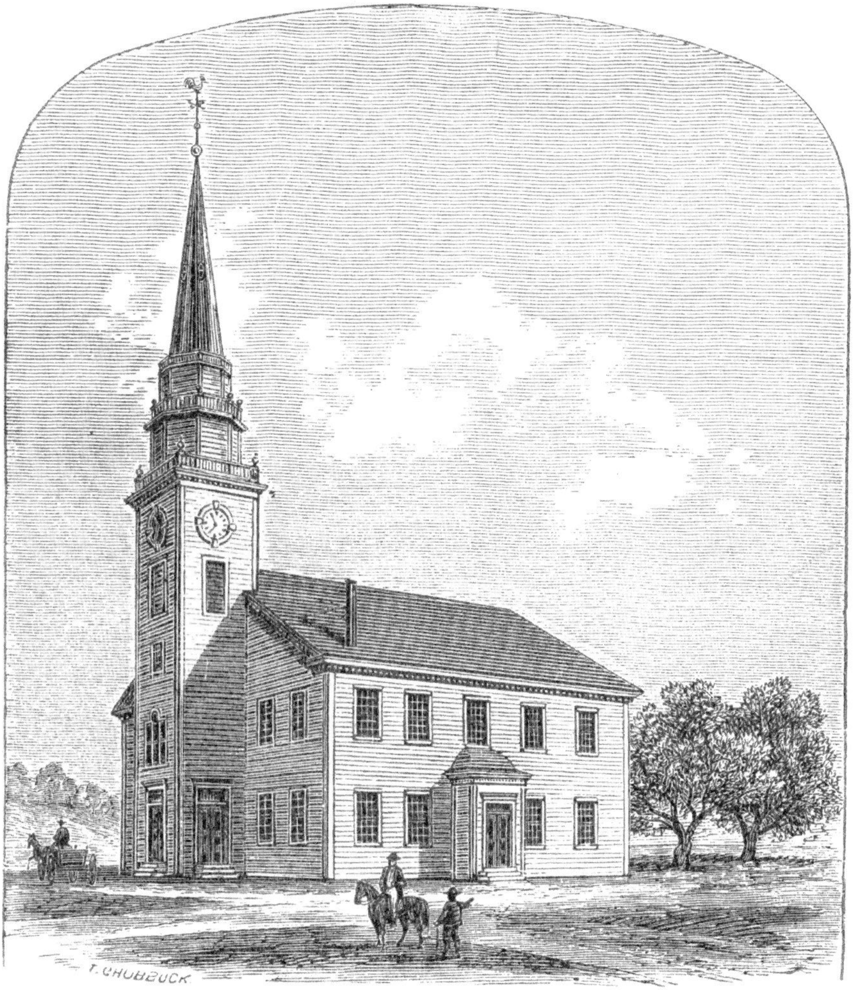


Illustration of the third meetinghouse. *From* King's Handbook of Springfield, *1884.*

members of the congregation, who ignored the pastors of the surrounding towns and offered Breck the position anyway.

The conflict came to a head on October 8, 1735, the planned day of Breck's ordination. At the request of the other Hampshire ministers, he wrote an orthodox confession of faith, but this did not satisfy some of his opponents, who instead had him arrested. They asserted that "he has broched and vented many articles of the Faith wholly subversive of the most Holy Faith of our Christian Religion, as well as been guilty of moral immoralities," and instead of being ordained that day, Breck spent the night in custody.

The matter was soon resolved, though, in favor of Breck. Connecticut, where he had allegedly made the blasphemous remarks, declined to take any action against him, and the Massachusetts House of Representatives expressed concern about civil authorities interfering with church matters in such a manner. He was ordained on January 27, 1736, and since no local pastors were willing to preach the ordination sermon, it was performed by William Cooper of Boston.

Breck's ministry in Springfield included the construction of a new meetinghouse, which began in 1749 and finished three years later. It was located on the western part of Court Square, directly in front of where the current Old First Church now stands. Its design was common for New England churches at the time, with a high pulpit, square pews and a main entrance on the long side of the building, facing Main Street. The steeple was on the side of the building facing Elm Street and was topped with the same rooster weathervane that is now on Old First Church.

In colonial New England, it was not unusual for a young pastor to remain in the same church for the rest of his life. In Longmeadow, Stephen Williams, who had been one of Breck's opponents in 1735, served his congregation for sixty-six years before his death in 1782, and Breck died two years later, after forty-nine years in the Springfield pulpit.

The following year, the church ordained Bezaleel Howard who, like Breck, was a young, theologically liberal Harvard graduate when he began his pastorate here. He resigned in 1803 due to poor health but continued preaching until the church found a replacement. It was around this time, though, that many Congregational churches in New England began to experience the divide between the orthodox Trinitarian and the liberal Unitarian beliefs, and here in Springfield it took six years and thirty-seven candidates before the congregation unanimously selected twenty-four-year-old Dartmouth graduate Samuel Osgood.

When he was ordained in 1809, Osgood was, like his predecessors, viewed as a liberal, but as the divide grew between the two factions, he aligned his doctrine with the more traditional Calvinist beliefs. The majority of the church supported him, but the Unitarians in the congregation were influential, wealthy and vocal. Hoping to avoid a church schism, parishioners asked for his resignation, with the intention of choosing a more moderate replacement. Osgood was unwavering, though, and in 1819, the Unitarians formed a new church, which became the Church of the Unity.

Despite the loss of some of its most prominent members, Osgood's congregation embarked on an ambitious building project to replace the

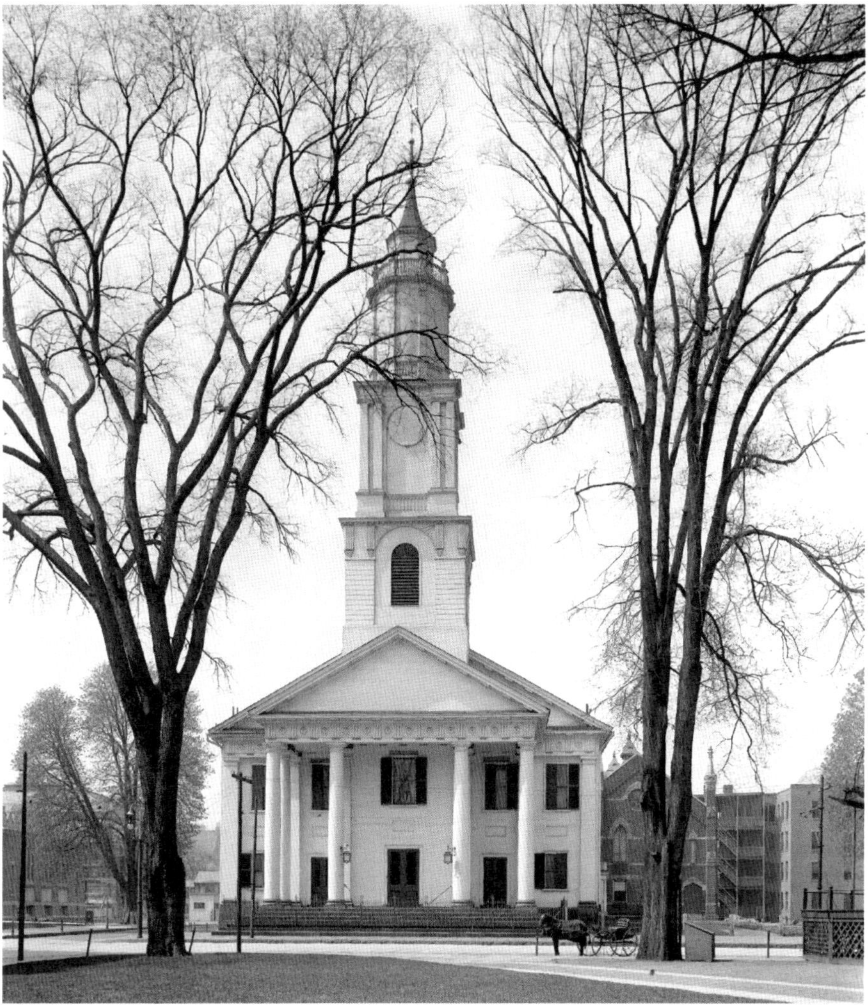

Old First Church, seen from Court Square around 1908. *Library of Congress.*

seventy-five-year-old meetinghouse. The result was the present-day Old First Church building, which was dedicated in August 1819. It was designed by Isaac Damon—who built a number of other western Massachusetts churches in the early 1800s—and reflects a combination of Federal and Greek Revival architecture. It is more elaborate than its predecessor, with columns supporting a triangular pediment over the front portico and a 125-foot, three-stage steeple above it.

Osgood remained at the new church building for the next thirty-five years, during which time Springfield grew from a town of under three thousand people in 1810 to a city of over twelve thousand by the time he retired in 1854. The church also grew, adding over one thousand new members during his pastorate.

Years after his death, in the church's 1915 history book, Osgood was recalled as having "stood fearlessly and without compromise for what he thought to be right, and was a power in the community." This included his staunch defense of orthodox beliefs early in his ministry, and it also included his strong opposition to slavery, which came to define much of his later career. He was one of the vice-presidents of the Hampden County Anti-Slavery Society, whose first meeting was held at Old First Church in 1838, and along with preaching against slavery, he played an active role in the Underground Railroad. His house, on the west side of Main Street between Howard and Union Streets, provided shelter for up to fifty runaway slaves each year. For those who chose to stay in Springfield instead of continuing to Canada, he taught them how to read and write and found employment for them.

The church building, which was often referred to as "Osgood's Meeting House," has remained a fixture in Court Square and is a reminder of the city's rich history. The interior has been renovated several times over the years, but the exterior has remained largely unchanged. However, the First Church congregation, which at 370 years old was one of the oldest in the state, no longer exists. It disbanded in 2007 amid declining membership and increased maintenance costs, but the city purchased the historic building to ensure its preservation and now rents it out for church services and other events.

## CHURCH OF THE UNITY

The Unitarians who left the First Church in 1819 soon built their own church on State Street, at what is now the corner of Willow Street. It was designed by Simon Sanborn in a Greek Revival style that bore some resemblance to Old First Church but was on a smaller scale. Jonathan Dwight Sr., one of the leaders of the Unitarians, paid for its construction, and it was dedicated on September 2, 1819, just two weeks after the completion of Old First Church. The following year, William B.O. Peabody was ordained as the first pastor of the church, which was originally named the Second Congregational Society in the First Parish

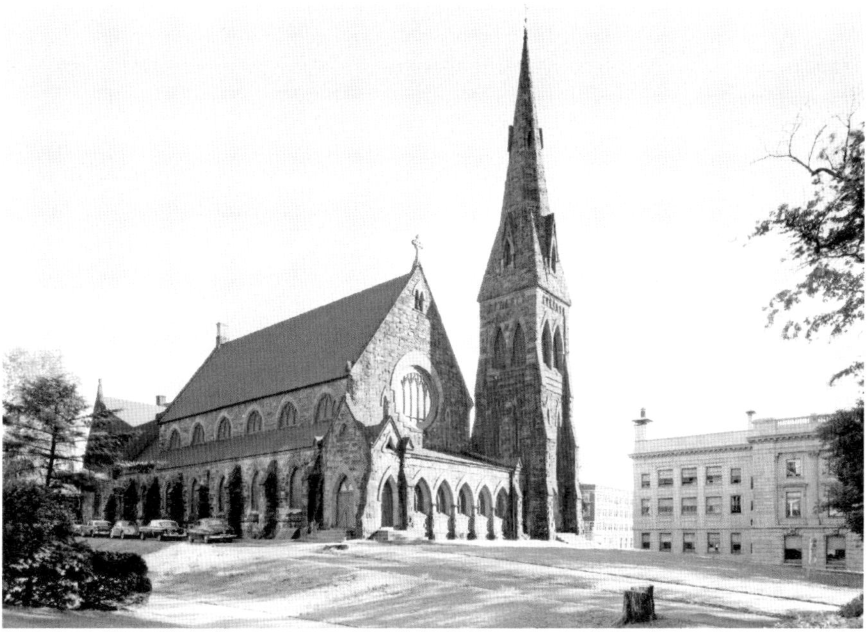

The Church of the Unity in 1959, two years before its demolition. *Library of Congress.*

in Springfield and later simplified to the Third Congregational Society in Springfield.

By the 1860s, the congregation was planning to build a new church, and in so doing, it inadvertently helped launch the career of one of the most prominent and influential American architects of the nineteenth century. At the time, Henry Hobson Richardson was an obscure young architect without any major commissions, but he was allowed to submit a design for the competition thanks to railroad executive Chester W. Chapin, whose son-in-law had been Richardson's classmate in college.

Even though Richardson was competing against far more established architects, his design was selected, and the building—dedicated in 1869 as the Church of the Unity—became his first major work. Its Gothic design is very different from the Romanesque Revival style that later defined his career, but it was met with praise by the people of Springfield. A few days before the church's dedication, the *Springfield Republican* noted the building's "finely proportioned exterior, with solid walls and spire of Longmeadow free stone," and "its Italian-Gothic architecture, so graceful, yet so dignified." The interior was equally impressive, in which "every detail in its relation to every other one shows a unity of design that is at once satisfactory and admirable." Overall, the writer was confident that "the vast majority will pronounce it a beautiful temple for the worship of God." Some fifteen years later, after Richardson had become an established architect, *King's Handbook of Springfield* noted that "its beauty and form and of decoration are almost universally admired, and have attracted much attention from travelers, as well as from those to whom they are more familiar."

Richardson soon earned other commissions, including the offices for Chapin's Western Railroad here in Springfield. Later in his career, as he established his Romanesque architecture, the style came to be known as Richardsonian Romanesque and was widely imitated by other architects. It did not take long, though, for his Church of the Unity to be copied here in the Springfield area. Just three years later, West Springfield's First Congregational Church was completed as a brick imitation of Richardson's design. Although it hardly compares to the original, it is still standing as an example of the architectural influence of the Church of the Unity.

The Church of the Unity was one of many new churches built on or near this section of State Street in the 1860s and 1870s, responding to the city's explosive growth in the post–Civil War era. At the time, its members primarily lived in the downtown area, but as the city's population shifted in

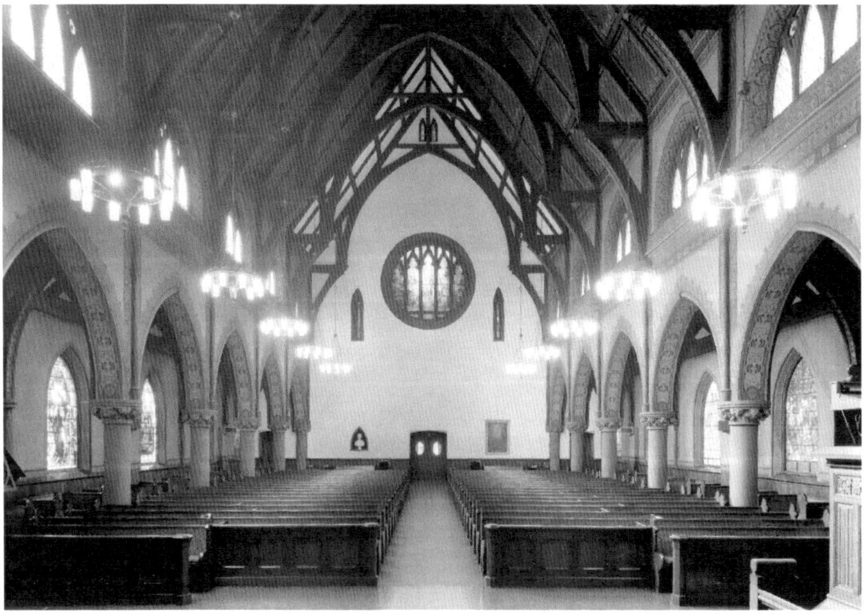

The interior of the Church of the Unity, 1959. *Library of Congress.*

the twentieth century, much of the congregation moved to the suburbs. The church, which was now Unitarian Universalist after its 1928 merger with St. Paul's Universalist Church, followed the members to the suburbs in the early 1960s.

The members sold the old building and opened a new one on Porter Lake Drive near Forest Park, taking the old organ with them and selling the stained-glass windows. Despite the historical and architectural value of the rest of the church, it was demolished in 1961 to make way for a planned apartment building. Ultimately, though, these apartments were never built, and over fifty years later, the site across the street from the Central Library remains vacant except for a parking lot.

## FIRST BAPTIST CHURCH

Around the same time that the Unitarians were forming their own church, other Christian denominations began to establish a foothold in Springfield, including Baptists. While the Unitarians were a split from within the existing Congregational Church, the Baptists were largely outsiders, brought to Springfield by the growing armory.

The Baptists organized their first church in 1811, with nineteen members who lived on the outskirts of town in the Watershops area. For the first ten years, the church led a nomadic existence, with neither a building nor a pastor. Members held their services in homes and schools until 1821, when they built their first meetinghouse at the corner of Central and Cherry Streets. Membership was up to about fifty at this point, and the following year, Allen Hough became the first permanent pastor. The Baptists also established Cherry Lane Cemetery next to their meetinghouse, where many of the founding members of the church are buried.

With membership continuing to grow, the church moved to a new location in 1832, at the corner of Maple and Mulberry Streets, and again in 1847 to the corner of Main Street and Harrison Avenue. Each move brought the Baptists closer to the center of Springfield, reflecting both their increasing size and status within the community. They remained at their Main Street location until 1887, at which point the church had over four hundred members. The city had also grown, too, and the church's location had become valuable commercial real estate,

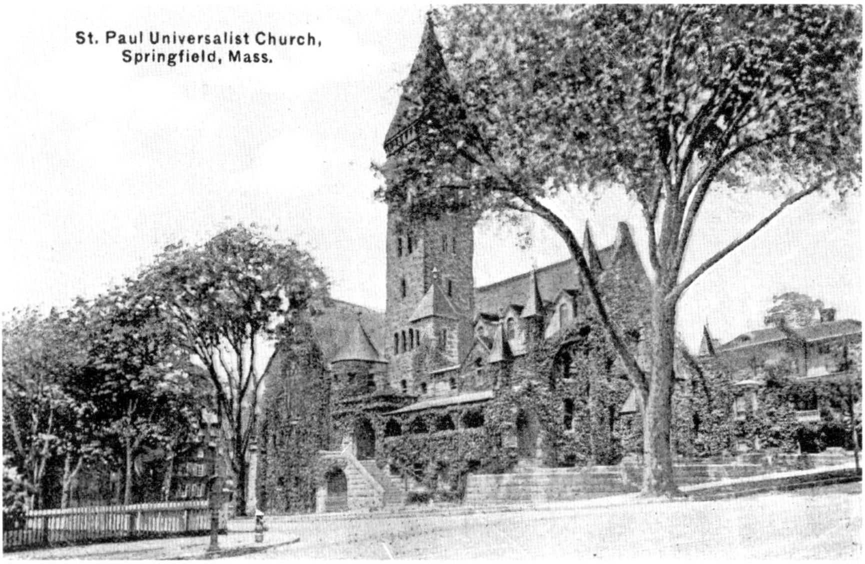


A postcard view of First Baptist Church from the 1910s, after it had become St. Paul's Universalist Church. *Author's collection.*

so in 1889, the congregation relocated to a new building at the corner of State and Spring Streets.

Here it joined the many other prominent churches along this section of State Street, with a building designed by New York architects Lawrence B. Valk & Son. Probably drawing inspiration from Henry Hobson Richardson's works, they incorporated many elements of Romanesque architecture into their design, including a Longmeadow brownstone exterior, plenty of arches and turrets and an off-center tower that stood 125 feet tall, the same height as the steeple of Old First Church. The main entrance was on the State Street side of the building, with an entry hall that led to a large vestry. This room was surrounded by four parlors, each of which had its own fireplace. Beyond the vestry, on the north side of the building, was the sanctuary, which had curved pews arranged in a semicircle around the pulpit area.

Another Baptist church, Highland Baptist Church, was built farther up State Street at the corner of Stebbins Street in 1893, but it burned down in 1906 in a deadly fire that claimed the lives of two firemen. Highland Baptist's congregation joined with First Baptist while its church was being rebuilt, and when the sanctuary was completed the following year, the two churches decided to formally merge. They left the eighteen-year-old building at Spring Street and moved into the new one, becoming First-Highland Baptist Church. They later returned to the First Baptist name after State Street Baptist Church joined in 1920, and the building, which is still standing, is now the home of Alden Baptist Church.

Following the merger, the old building was sold to St. Paul's Universalist Church, which moved here from its former location at the corner of Bridge and Chestnut Streets. After St. Paul's joined the Church of the Unity in 1928, the building was sold to the Knights of Columbus, who renovated it into a clubhouse.

Around 1948, the old church was demolished to build a parking garage for the adjacent Federal Land Bank building. Parts of the church walls were incorporated into the garage, including one wall that is still visible from Spring Street on the north side of the structure. Much of the remaining brownstone from the church was salvaged and used to build a new parish house for South Congregational Church, which is still standing behind the church along High Street. This recycling of building materials allowed the addition to match the rest of the church, which was built with stone from the same quarry as First Baptist Church.

# 2
# TRANSPORTATION

Transportation has always played a major role in Springfield's development. Unlike most other colonial towns of the Connecticut River Valley, Springfield was not settled as a farming community, and agriculture has never been a significant part of the city's economy. However, Springfield's founder, William Pynchon, saw it as an ideal location for a trading center.

Springfield is situated along the Connecticut River, which provides a natural north–south route through the western part of New England, and two major rivers flow into the Connecticut River: the Chicopee River to the east and the Westfield River to the west. These rivers provided natural trading routes in all four cardinal directions, and long before European colonists arrived there was already a network of Native American trails through here.

## Old Toll Bridge

As beneficial as the Connecticut River was to Springfield's trade, it was also a major obstacle. At over one thousand feet wide, the river was well beyond the reach of colonial bridge builders, so for the first 170 years, the only way across was by boat. Early settlers crossed in simple dugout canoes, and eventually, three regular ferries were established across the river: York Street, Elm Street and present-day Liberty Street.

There was certainly enough traffic to and from Springfield to justify a bridge, but building it would be a daunting task. Aside from its width, the Connecticut River was a challenge because of ice—which could easily knock a bridge off its piers—and spring freshets, when the melted snow from Vermont, New Hampshire and northern Massachusetts flooded the river.

The first bridge across any part of the four-hundred-mile-long Connecticut River was built in 1785 at Bellows Falls, Vermont, one hundred miles upstream of Springfield. There, the river passes through a narrow gorge less than 250 feet wide, making it an ideal place for a bridge. Because of the depth of the gorge, ice and floods were not threats, and the bridge's only pier was built on a large exposed rock in the middle of the river.

Springfield, of course, had none of these advantages, but even in the 1780s, there was talk of building a bridge. Reportedly, when Reverend Bezaleel Howard predicted that it would happen, one prominent citizen remarked "Parson Howard talks like a fool." Another skeptic is quoted in the 1884 *King's Handbook of Springfield* as having said "Gentlemen, you might as well undertake to bridge the Atlantic Ocean."

By the turn of the nineteenth century, the bridge was starting to become a reality. The first challenge, though, was building five stone piers in the middle of the river to support the bridge. Israel Reed of Harvard, Massachusetts, was hired to construct the piers, each of which was made up of about two thousand tons of stone and had to be supported with piles driven into the riverbed. In the days before steam power, this work was done with horses, and *King's Handbook of Springfield* provides a description of the work involved:

> *A large floating platform was constructed, and anchored in the river near the site fixed for a pier; on it was placed the necessary machinery for raising the hammer; this was operated by a horse winding a rope around a drum, or cylinder. This horse "swung around the circle" from morning till night, from Monday till Saturday, and from spring till early winter; but no man has numbered the revolutions he performed, nor the thousands of miles he travelled during the process. On the platform was a stable for his shelter and repose at night; for he slept on the "bosom of the deep," not being taken ashore till the close of work for winter.*

Along with the bridge piers, two other piers were built just upstream of the bridge. These were designed so that large ice sheets floating downstream would ride up onto the piers and break apart, instead of riding up onto the bridge piers and breaking the bridge apart.

The work of building the bridge itself was done by Jonathan Wolcott of Windham, Connecticut. It was uncovered and consisted of six arched spans, with the roadway built directly atop the arches so that travelers had to walk up and down about six feet on each arch as they crossed the bridge. The arches made it safer for heavy wagons to cross because of the added strength, while at the same time made it more difficult for them to cross because of the uneven bridge deck.

His design was praised by contemporary newspapers such as the *Haverhill Museum*, which declared, "The bridge is pronounced by connoisseurs in architecture to be one of the best of its kind in America; combining in its appearance, elegance and neatness with strength and durability." Many years later, though, as bridge architecture advanced, Mason A. Green would describe it in his book *Springfield, 1636–1886* as a "clumsy and indeed grotesque structure."

There was at least one fatal accident during the construction of the bridge. In September 1805, as the bridge was nearing completion, part of the falsework collapsed as several workers were carrying a large plank across it. The men were injured by both the forty-foot fall and the falling debris from the bridge, and one of them, forty-year-old Revolutionary War veteran Amos Snow, was killed.

The bridge opened less than two months after this incident, with West Springfield pastor Joseph Lathrop preaching the dedication sermon. Around three thousand people, more than Springfield's entire population at the time, attended the ceremony, and the bridge was opened to the public toll-free on the first day. After the first day, tolls were charged based on the amount of wear and tear put on the bridge. Sheep and swine could cross for one cent, foot passengers for three cents and a horse and rider for seven cents. Vehicles cost more, with the most expensive being thirty-three cents for four-wheeled carriages.

Despite glowing reports about its strength and durability, though, the first bridge lasted less than ten years. Uncovered wooden bridges tend to have a short lifespan because the structural elements are exposed to the weather, and this, combined with heavy traffic from the Springfield Armory during the War of 1812, weakened the bridge. It collapsed in 1814, and for several years, Springfield was again without a bridge.

As with the first bridge, the construction of the second was partially funded by lottery. For $6, a substantial sum in 1815, individuals had a chance to win the $15,000 grand prize or one of several smaller prizes. The lottery ended up paying for about half of the $22,000 construction costs, and the bridge opened on October 1, 1816.

The second bridge was designed by Isaac Damon, who built Springfield's Old First Church less than two years later. Unlike the first bridge, Damon's was covered, to protect its structural elements, and it was built on seven piers instead of five. The additional piers allowed each span to be shorter, which meant the bridge deck could be built level instead of as a series of arches.

Although it was far better protected from structural decay, this bridge lasted less than a year and a half. Unseasonably warm weather in early March 1818 had flooded the river with melted snow, dislodging a one- to two-foot-thick sheet of ice just upstream of the bridge. Five of the piers collapsed under the weight of the ice and the force of the river, and most of the bridge was swept away, leaving only a few spans on the West Springfield side of the river.

The bridge committee again turned to a lottery to raise money for the repairs. It published an almost desperate plea to the public in the *Hampden Federalist*, writing, "[W]e cannot but hope, therefore, that the public spirit of the inhabitants will be fully exhibited in the purchase of Tickets in this

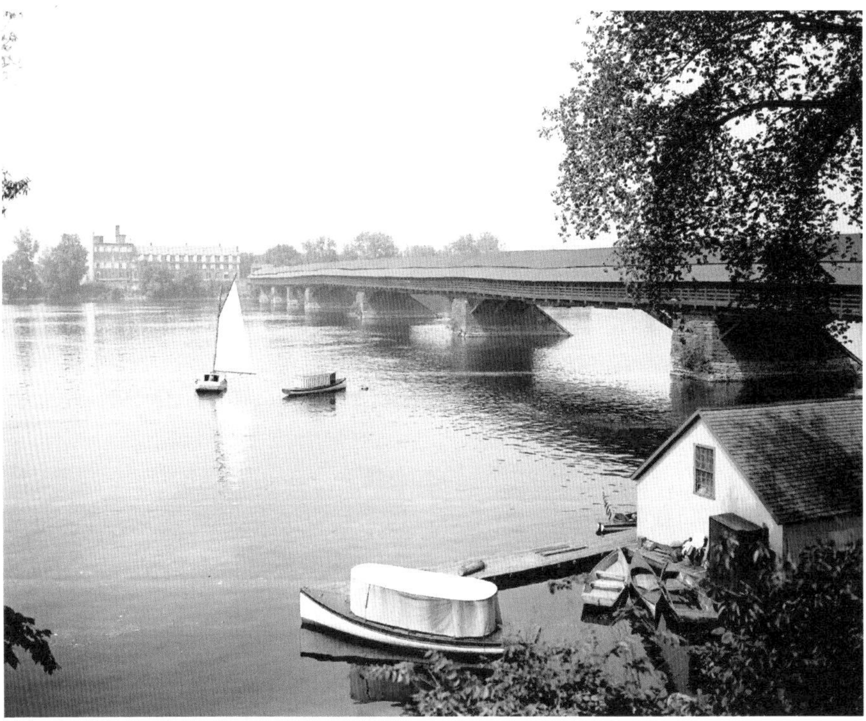

The Old Toll Bridge, seen from the downstream side looking across the river toward West Springfield, around 1900–10. *Library of Congress.*

Excellent Lottery, which *may* make them rich, and *will* eventually be a means of reestablishing a permanent bridge across the river at this place."

Many of the stones and timbers from the bridge were salvaged and incorporated into the new one, and the rebuilt structure opened in 1820. It turned out to be far more permanent than probably any of the committee members could have imagined, although it was never particularly profitable as a toll bridge. The bridge was finally sold to Hampden County in 1872, and the tolls were eliminated.

The Old Toll Bridge, as it came to be known, remained the only bridge across the Connecticut River in Springfield until the construction of the North End Bridge in 1877 and the South End Bridge two years later. These two iron-truss bridges were far more modern than the old covered wooden bridge, but it survived well into the age of automobiles. The Springfield Street Railway even installed tracks and operated a horse-drawn trolley line over the bridge, which was used from 1887 to 1891 before the system switched to electric trolleys and crossed the North End Bridge instead.

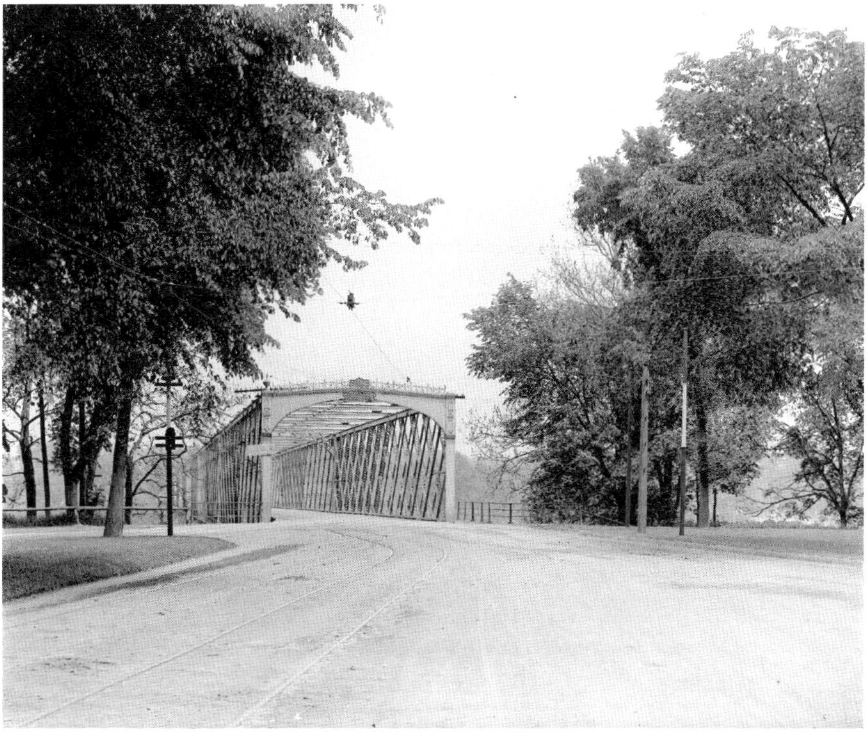

The original North End Bridge from the West Springfield side, around 1900–10. *Library of Congress.*

The end finally came in 1922, with the completion of the Memorial Bridge. The 102-year-old bridge was then dismantled, and today, the only trace of its existence are two streets on opposite sides of the river. Both Springfield and West Springfield have a Bridge Street, and although neither one leads to a bridge anymore, they mark where the Old Toll Bridge once crossed the river.

For Springfield, though, the Memorial Bridge could not have been completed at a better time. Just a year later, the North End Bridge was destroyed in a fire, and the Memorial Bridge had to handle all its automobile and trolley traffic until the present North End Bridge opened in 1925. Just after the fire, the *Republican* commented on the irony of the situation, pointing out that while the Old Toll Bridge was "a veritable tinder box in its wooden construction, with dry timbers and dusty and splintered planks," it survived for over a century, yet the modern iron North End Bridge was destroyed by a fire in under fifty years.

## Union Station

Before even the first bridge across the Connecticut River had been built, there were already proposals for far more ambitious transportation improvements. Although Springfield is only eighty miles from Boston, there is no direct water route, and overland transportation was difficult in eighteenth-century Massachusetts. Perhaps no man knew this better than Henry Knox, who led a six-week journey from Fort Ticonderoga in New York to Boston in the winter of 1775–76, bringing much-needed artillery to the Continental army.

His journey across the Berkshires through Springfield was ultimately successful, but he probably had this experience in mind sixteen years later when he was serving as the secretary of war. In order to better link Boston to the western parts of the state, he proposed a canal from Boston to the Connecticut River in Springfield. Massachusetts granted him a charter for his canal in 1792, but Knox evidently dropped the idea after some initial surveys were done.

Over thirty years later, Massachusetts conducted another survey of a possible canal route from Boston to Albany. With an estimated cost of $6 million, this plan never advanced beyond the surveys either, but in 1827, the state legislature took a different approach and examined the possibility of a railroad between the two cities.

As with the bridge, there were plenty who scoffed at the idea, but within eight years, Boston and Worcester were linked by rail. By 1837, work had begun on the Western Railroad, which would continue west from Worcester to Albany via Springfield. The line was completed as far as Springfield in 1839, with a celebration that included a number of dignitaries, including Massachusetts governor Edward Everett, former governor and Congressman Levi Lincoln, Congressman William B. Calhoun and future congressmen George Ashmun and Amasa Walker.

The opening of the railroad turned out to be a momentous occasion for Springfield. Long a major transportation hub because of its rivers and roads, it would now play a major role in the nation's railroad network. Railroads were still in their infancy in America, but Governor Everett, as the keynote speaker at the ceremony, observed how Massachusetts was "on the verge of the most stupendous network of intercommunication ever woven by the hands of man." He predicted that, aside from the signing of the Declaration of Independence and the Constitution, "that day will be most auspicious in the annals of Massachusetts, when the Western hills and the Eastern waves shall be brought together—and a bond of connection, commercial, political, and social, shall bind the extremities of the Commonwealth in a union never to be dissolved."

Others went even further in their recognition of this railroad's significance. While Everett spoke of linking western Massachusetts to Boston, British author James Silk Buckingham wrote in 1842 that the newly completed line from Boston to Albany was just the first step, "with a prospect of extending the line from thence to the Rocky Mountains, and beyond these again to the Pacific." Although the transcontinental railroad was still over twenty-five years in the future, Buckingham concluded by asking, "With such a population, such governors, and such enterprises as these, what may not the United States, led on by those of New England, achieve?"

Not many of the dignitaries present at the ceremony would live to see the completion of the transcontinental railroad, but it did not take long for Springfield to become a major railroad crossroads. The line through the Berkshires to Albany was completed in 1841, and three years later, the Hartford & Springfield Railroad opened along the Connecticut River, providing rail service south to Hartford and New Haven and steamboat connections to New York City. Around the same time, the Connecticut River Railroad was built along the river north from Springfield, reaching Northampton in 1845, Greenfield in 1846 and Vernon, Vermont, in 1849.

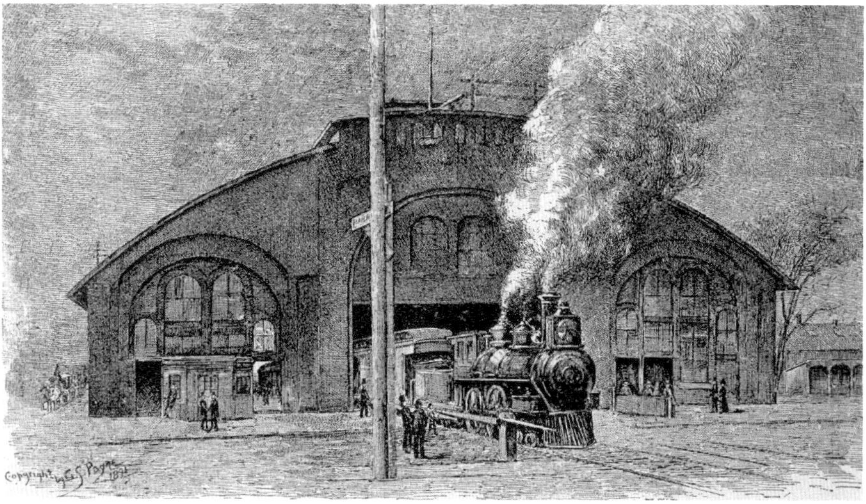

Illustration of the 1851 depot as it appeared from Main Street. *From* Picturesque Hampden, *1892.*

Springfield's first railroad station was located just west of Main Street and made of wood. It stood until 1851, when sparks from a passing locomotive started a fire that destroyed the building. It was replaced with a large, shed-like structure made of red brick and iron. Like the first one, it was covered and was built directly over the tracks, so that trains had to travel through the four-hundred-foot length of the station. Within the building, there were separate stations on either side. On the north side of the tracks was the station for the Connecticut River Railroad and westbound Western Railroad trains, and on the south side was the Springfield & Hartford and the eastbound Western Railroad trains.

The station was designed by George William Whistler, a railroad engineer who was possibly the least-known member of his family. He was the oldest son of George Washington Whistler, who had been the chief engineer of the Western Railroad a decade earlier, when the line was built from Springfield to Albany. Two of his half-brothers also overshadowed him; William McNeill Whister served as a Confederate surgeon in the Civil War, and James Abbott McNeill Whistler became one of the leading American painters of the second half of the nineteenth century.

Whistler's station changed ownership in 1867 when the Western Railroad and the Boston & Worcester were consolidated into the Boston & Albany Railroad. The station was less than twenty years old at the time, but there was already an obvious need for a newer one. Springfield had more than doubled in population between 1850 and 1870, and surrounding communities such as Holyoke and Chicopee had become major manufacturing centers. All of this put a strain on the old station, but compounding the problem was the disruption that it caused for traffic on Main Street. The station was located just a short distance west of Main Street, with the tracks crossing directly over the street. Between arriving and departing trains and switching activity from the rail yard, the gates on Main Street were usually closed as often as they were open, and one observer in 1872 counted sixty-six times that the street was closed on a given day between 11:00 a.m. and 3:00 p.m.

In 1869, the state legislature authorized the Boston & Albany Railroad to build a new station and raise the railroad above street level, but the next twenty years were spent arguing over the specifics before any work was done. The city and the railroad could not agree on how much of the costs each side needed to cover, the city could not figure out which department had the authority to make a decision and hotel and store owners in the area were concerned about how their properties would be affected by the raising of the railroad and the lowering of the street. There were also disagreements over whether the new station should be located west of Main Street, where it had always been, or east of Main Street, where there would be more room.

The delays continued until 1887, when the citizens of Springfield appealed to the state board of railroad commissioners. After holding a hearing with concerned citizens and railroad representatives, the board concluded that the station was far from adequate and recommended that a new one be built to the east of Main Street, with a bridge to carry the tracks over the

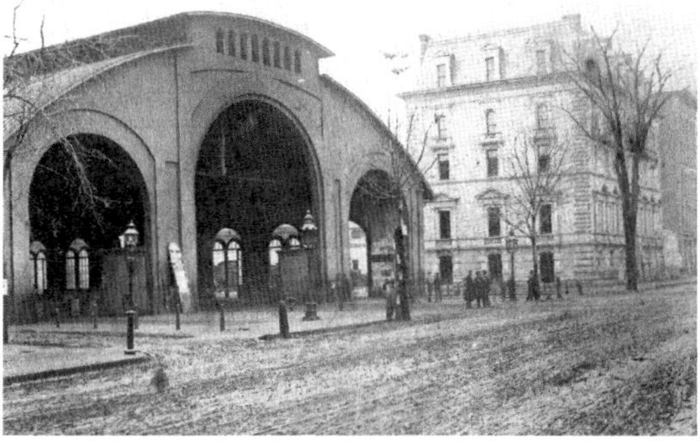

The old depot with the notorious Main Street crossing, around the 1870s or 1880s. *Boston Public Library*.

street. It also addressed the fears of businessmen in the area, noting that any effects on property values would be minimal and would be far outweighed by the benefits to the city. In illustrating the absurdity of such fears, the board asserted, "Springfield is an enterprising and progressive city, and its Main Street is not to be permanently damaged because a railroad station is to be removed from it, or because it is no longer obstructed by trains on a level crossing."

Along with these long-term improvements, the board also made some suggestions on actions that the railroad could take immediately to address the concerns of the citizens. Perhaps chief among these was a recommendation that no freight train switching should be done across Main Street unless absolutely necessary. This certainly would not eliminate the traffic problems caused by the railroad crossing, but it would address one of the primary complaints that Springfield had been expressing for several decades.

However, the board's recommendations to the railroad were merely recommendations; only an act by the state legislature could force them to do anything. Almost a year after their report was issued, no work had been done on a new station, and the railroad was still switching freight cars across Main Street. Either of these issues could have been tolerable on their own, but the problem for Springfield was that they were inextricably tied together. The railroad could not raise the tracks without building a new station, and the board could not build a new station unless it knew for sure whether or not the tracks would be raised.

In the meantime, railroad traffic continued to increase. An advertisement in a December 1887 issue of the *Springfield Republican* listed all of the daily departures from Springfield, including fourteen eastbound and nine westbound Boston & Albany trains, fourteen southbound New York, New Haven & Hartford trains and twenty-five northbound Connecticut River Railroad trains, for a total of at least sixty-two passenger trains. This number does not include the many freight trains that passed through here, nor does it count the number of times that switching locomotives crossed Main Street while moving freight cars in the nearby rail yard.

The railroad and the city finally reached an agreement in February 1888, and it was approved by the county commissioners in May. Under the terms, the railroad would assume the cost of raising the tracks, and the city would lower Main Street by four feet and settle any damage claims brought by property owners. The railroad estimated its share of the costs, not counting a new station, to be around $200,000, while the

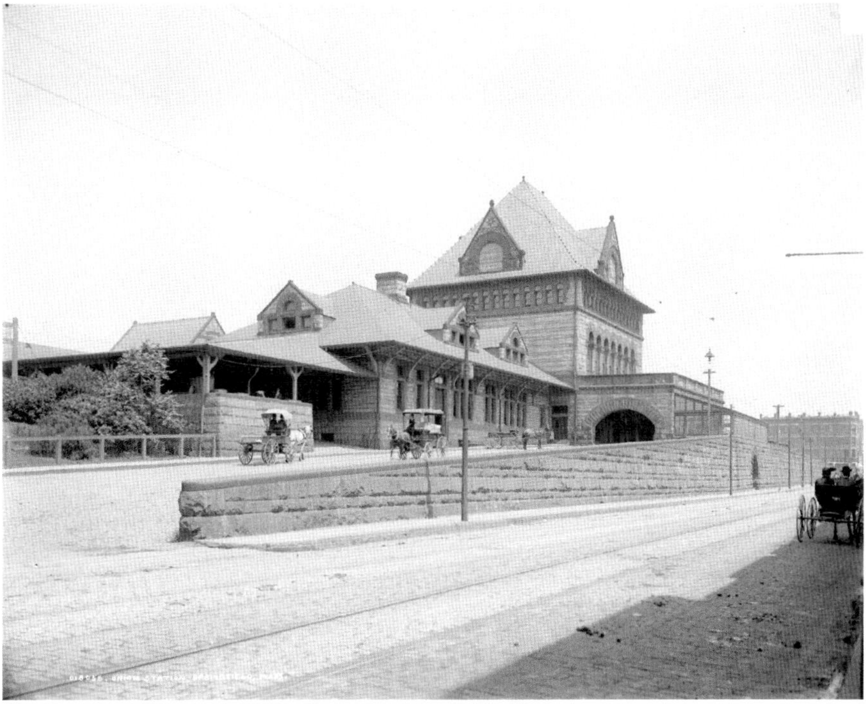

Union Station, seen from Lyman Street around 1905. *Library of Congress.*

city engineer estimated that Springfield would be responsible for about $84,000. It would not be an easy task, though; the work of demolishing the old station, building a new one, raising a half mile of tracks between Chestnut Street and the Connecticut River and building a stone arch bridge over Main Street all had to be done while minimizing disruptions to railroad and street traffic.

The old station was demolished in the spring of 1889, leaving only the platforms and two waiting rooms for passengers until the new station opened across the street in July. It was built based on the designs of Henry Hobson Richardson, who had been hired to design a number of stations along the Boston & Albany Railroad. After his death in 1886, his successors, Shepley, Rutan & Coolidge, completed many of these stations, including the one in Springfield.

With the new Union Station, Springfield finally had a grand railroad station worthy of the growing city's status. In the heyday of passenger rail travel, the railroad station was the first place in a city that visitors saw, and in Springfield, they arrived in a building that the *Springfield Republican*

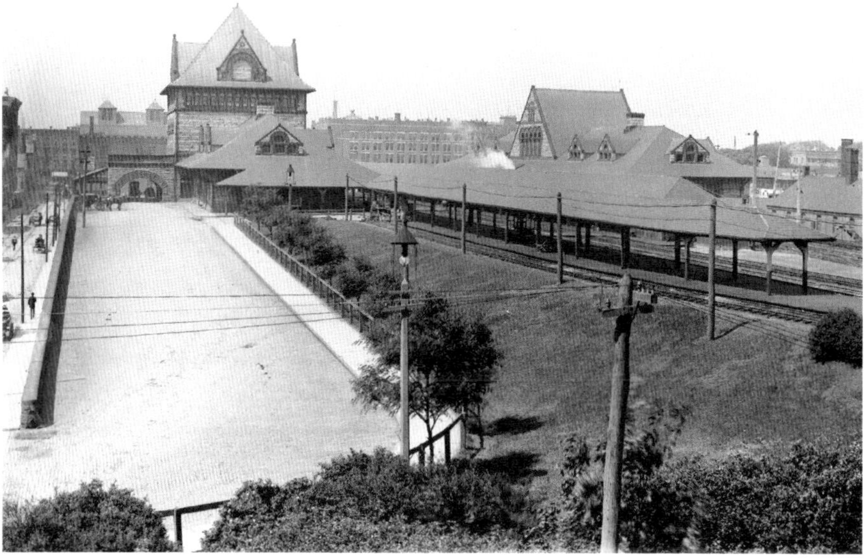

Union Station around 1900–10, showing the separate station buildings on each side of the tracks. *Library of Congress*.

later described as having "a monumental quality" and "a dignity and beauty making it comparable almost to a cathedral." However, it did not completely follow Richardson's original designs. His plans had called for a single station building on the south side and a large train shed covering the tracks, but in the end, the train shed was abandoned. Due to objections from the Connecticut River Railroad, it was redesigned with separate stations on either side of the tracks. Like its predecessor, the south tracks served passengers traveling south and east, with the north side serving those heading north and west. Each station building had its own ticket offices and waiting rooms, and they were separated by four tracks and three platforms.

This change would turn out to be a major design flaw, and it helped contribute to the station's relatively short lifespan. By dividing the station in two, it reduced the amount of passenger waiting room space by adding redundant features such as ticket offices on both sides. There was also no walkway under the tracks, so passengers had to cross four busy through tracks in order to get to the other side of the station. Having stations on either side also prevented any additional tracks or platforms from being added, which became a major problem as passenger travel continued to grow.

Many of the railroad stations designed by Richardson and by Shepley, Rutan & Coolidge are still standing over a century later, but Springfield's Union Station is not one of them. Within about fifteen years of its completion, it was already obsolete; as early as 1906, the *Springfield Republican* was calling for its replacement. Increasing freight and passenger traffic, along with the station's size and layout, combined to cause delays on the railroads and made the station crowded and dangerous.

In retrospect, the station was an excellent example of Romanesque architecture from the late nineteenth century, and had it been preserved, it undoubtedly would have become a prominent historic landmark in Springfield. Even before its demolition it was praised for its architectural value, but there were few calls for its preservation, with the *Springfield Republican* observing in 1921 that "there seems to be, in fact, a nearly

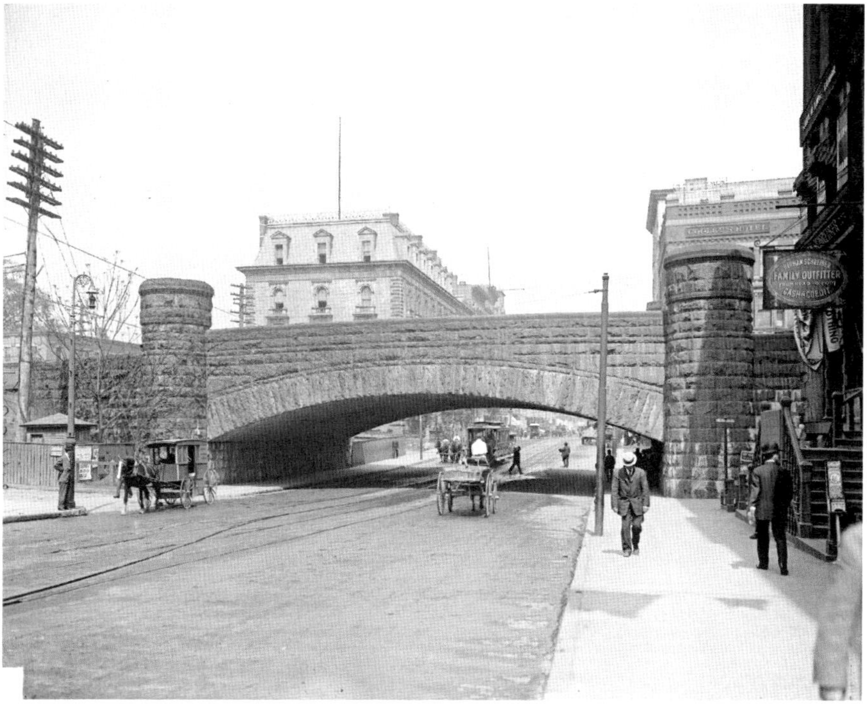


The railroad arch over Main Street, seen looking north around 1900–10, with the offices of the Boston and Albany Railroad in the distance. *Library of Congress.*

unanimous demand that the structure be cast to the scrapheap." Four years later, with its demolition at hand, the newspaper wrote that the station, "long execrated for its combination of discomfort, dinginess and danger, comes to the end of its career unlamented."

Ultimately, the practical value of a new station far outweighed the architectural merit of the old one, and by 1918, the railroad had drawn up plans for a new station. No further action was taken until after a November 1922 fire that started in the basement of the north side of the station. There were no injuries, and valuables such as mail, express packages and the ticket office cash were saved by railroad employees and an off-duty police officer. However, it caused about $25,000 worth of damage to the building and gave the railroad a reason to finally build the new station, which was officially authorized less than a month later.

The old station was demolished in stages starting in 1925, and the long-awaited new Union Station opened on December 19, 1926. Unlike its predecessor, it was no architectural marvel. From the exterior, it looked more like an ordinary office building than a grand railroad station, but on the inside it offered everything that the previous one had lacked. It was entirely on the north side of the tracks, with a large concourse, a waiting room and amenities such as a restaurant, soda fountain, barbershop, newsstand and shoe shine service. Along with accommodating far more passengers, it was also much easier for them to move around the station, with a tunnel under the railroad that connected to the Lyman Street side, allowing access to the station from the south without having to cross over the tracks. To prevent delays on the railroad, the number of tracks was increased from four to eleven, and each platform had staircases connecting to the tunnel under the tracks.

The new Union Station was designed to accommodate any future growth in passenger rail travel, but as it turned out, by the mid-twentieth century, the industry was in decline. Amtrak took over passenger service in 1971, and two years later, most of the old station was closed off. A new Amtrak station was built into the tunnel under the tracks, and the Lyman Street side became the station's only entrance. However, in 2010, work began on renovating the historic building and restoring it as a major regional transportation center. The station's old baggage handling building was demolished as part of the project and replaced with a parking garage and bus terminal. The main building has been rehabilitated after decades of neglect.

# SPRINGFIELD STREET RAILWAY

By the 1860s, Springfield had been connected to the outside world by railroads heading in all four compass directions, but it had very little for public transportation within the city. There were three horse-drawn omnibus lines at the time, but some of the city's business leaders were already envisioning a better system. In 1868, Chester W. Chapin, one of the wealthiest men in the city, and Henry Alexander, a former mayor, proposed a street railway system with horse-drawn trolleys that would run on tracks in the middle of the city streets. They were unable to convince enough investors to join, though, and abandoned their plan.

Another businessman, George Atwater, saw the potential of such a plan, and took over where Chapin and Alexander had left off. He had similar trouble attracting investors, as well as convincing city officials that the plan was practical. The board of aldermen laughed as it granted him permission to build the railway, members even taking up a collection among themselves and presenting him with a mock investment of eleven cents, which Atwater dutifully deposited into a bank account.

Construction began in the summer of 1869, but the ever-problematic Main Street railroad crossing complicated the project. The railroad objected to the street railway tracks crossing theirs, citing safety concerns, and the *Springfield Republican* paraphrased one pro-railroad alderman, who "didn't think it wise to inconvenience the public for a one-horse railroad, a mere little pony railroad." The board of aldermen ultimately voted in favor of Atwater, though, as did the Massachusetts Supreme Judicial Court, and the street railway opened in March 1870.

Initially, the railway had four cars and twenty-four horses, which were stabled in the North End at the corner of Main and Hooker Streets. From here, the line went south on Main Street to State Street and then east on State Street to Oak Street, for a total route of about two and a half miles. The first cars were small, measuring ten to twelve feet, and could seat around twelve people. They were pulled by a single horse, but as the cars and ridership grew, this was increased to two horses and then four for rush-hour trips. Fares were originally set at eight cents, or sixteen tickets for one dollar.

In its first year, over 250,000 passengers traveled on the Springfield Street Railway, and this increased as the system was expanded. In 1873, a new line was added through the South End, along Main Street from State Street to the Mill River, and the next year, the original line was extended east to

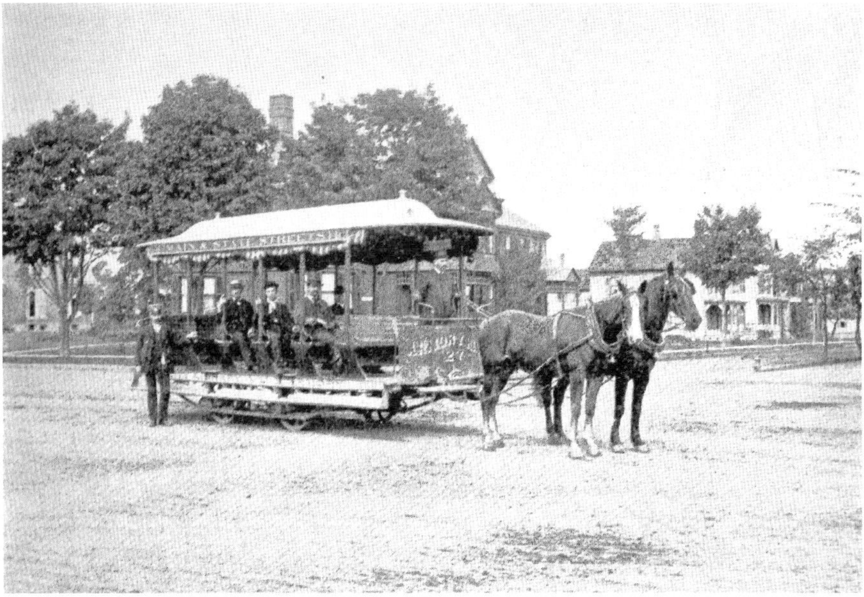

A horse-drawn trolley of the Springfield Street Railway, 1870s. *From* Springfield Present and Prospective, *1905.*

Winchester Square and north to Wason Avenue. Another new line was added in 1879 along Maple and Central Streets, connecting State Street to the Watershops. As the lines expanded, ticket prices fell, and in 1880, a single fare was reduced to six cents, or five tickets for twenty-five cents. By 1883, the company had an annual ridership of over 1 million, and the once-derided company had become a profitable investment.

The most significant change to the system came in 1890, when the company began replacing the horse-drawn cars with electric trolleys. By the next summer, all of the lines were electrified, and to save money on electricity costs the company built its own powerhouse next to the river at the foot of Margaret Street. It also built a new trolley barn in 1897 at the corner of Main and Carew Streets, which served as the company headquarters and supplemented the facility at Hooker Street.

During this time, the Springfield Street Railway helped to bring growth to the city, raising real estate values and spurring residential development along its routes. By the turn of the century, trolleys connected the growing Forest Park neighborhood with the rest of the city, with lines along Fort Pleasant Avenue, Belmont Avenue, White Street and Sumner Avenue. Indian Orchard, long isolated from the rest of the city, was connected by trolleys along Berkshire Avenue, and the North End had trolleys on Plainfield,

Main, Chestnut and Liberty Streets. The trolleys also brought people into the city from surrounding cities and towns, with direct routes to Holyoke, Northampton, Westfield, Palmer and Hartford

In 1904, the company's ridership increased to nearly nineteen million passengers, with 227 trolleys operating on ninety-four miles of track, including nearly fifty miles in Springfield alone. At the time, automobiles were just starting to come into existence, but the future of electric trolleys still seemed secure. In the decade that followed, even as automobiles became more accessible to the middle class, ridership more than doubled to over forty-four million a year by 1916. Three years later, the *Springfield Republican* reported on a hearing regarding the future of Springfield Street Railway, in which an expert "declared before the commission that nothing can take the place of the street railway." He argued that, although buses existed in some cities, they were not usually profitable because electricity was much cheaper than gasoline.

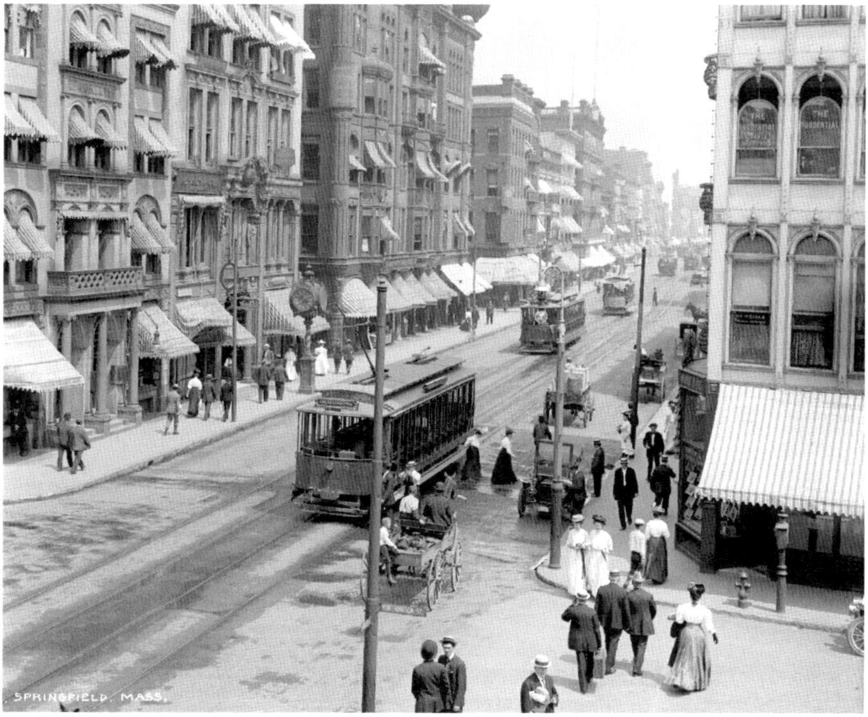


Main Street trolleys, seen looking south from the corner of Worthington Street around 1908. *Library of Congress.*

However, just over twenty years later, the electric trolleys that had been a common sight in Springfield for half a century were replaced with buses. Amid much fanfare, the last two trolleys made their final run in the early morning hours of June 24, 1940, on a trip from the North End to the X at Forest Park and then back up to the Hooker Street trolley barn. By the time the trolleys made their return trip up Main Street at 1:30 a.m., they were followed by around one hundred cars, with horns honking and crowds cheering. On board the trolleys, no fares were charged, and the passengers worked on collecting souvenirs, including removing the advertisements and cutting down the leather straps.

The Springfield Street Railway continued to operate buses in Springfield for many years, but like many other public transit systems in the country, it became unprofitable and dependent on government subsidies. By 1981, its garage and buses had been sold to the Pioneer Valley Transit Authority (PVTA), which has provided public transportation in Springfield ever since. There are a few reminders of the old company, though, including the 1897 trolley barn, which still stands at Memorial Square. Farther up Main Street is another trolley barn, located on the site of George Atwater's original 1869 stables at the corner of Hooker Street. Built in 1916, it was later converted into a bus garage and remains in use by the PVTA as a storage and repair facility.

3

# GOVERNMENT

Springfield was established in 1636 as the first colonial settlement in western Massachusetts. For the next two centuries, it had a town form of government, with a board of selectmen and a town meeting. In 1855, it was incorporated as a city, and since then the city government has been housed in several different buildings.

Along with town and city government, Springfield has also been home to county courthouses for most of its existence. From 1662 to 1794, it was the seat of Hampshire County, and since 1812, it has been the seat of Hampden County. During this time, there have been four different permanent courthouses in Springfield, all in the immediate vicinity of the present-day Court Square.

## Colonial Courthouse

County government came to Springfield in 1662, when it was made the shire town of the newly created Hampshire County. The county included the three Connecticut River towns of Springfield, Northampton and Hadley, with vaguely defined borders that extended up to thirty miles beyond the towns. Although Springfield had been designated as the county seat, the court sessions alternated between Springfield and Northampton, and for many years, neither town had a dedicated courthouse.

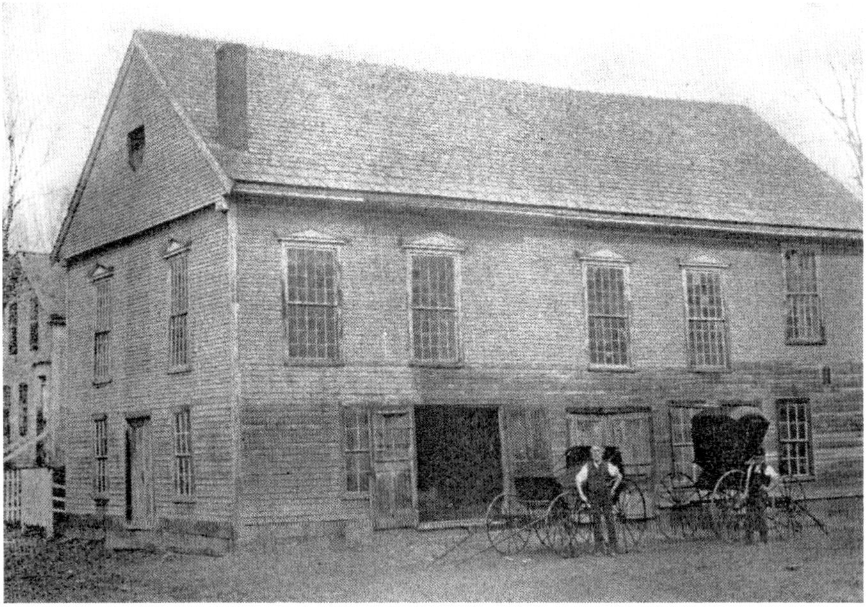

The old 1723 courthouse during its time as a carriage shop on Sanford Street around the 1860s. *From* Picturesque Hampden, *1892.*

The first permanent courthouse was built in Springfield in 1723, and it originally stood on the east side of Main Street, opposite present-day Court Square. This plain, two-story wooden building remained in use as the county courthouse until 1794, when the seat of Hampshire County was moved to Northampton.

During its time as a courthouse, this building played a role in several important events in American history. Following the Intolerable Acts of 1774, it was the scene of an anti-British mob, and less than a year later, in March 1775, another mob prevented the court from meeting by blocking the judges and sheriff from entering.

Just a decade later, the courthouse was again at the center of controversy, in what became known as Shays' Rebellion. At the end of the American Revolution, much of the economy in western Massachusetts consisted of small-scale subsistence farming, in contrast to the wealthy merchants and their political allies in the eastern part of the state. Since cash was scarce, these farmers frequently purchased goods from merchants on credit and paid their debts with crops from their farms.

This system worked until after the war, when British creditors began demanding cash from American merchants. The merchants then passed this demand on to the farmers and required them to repay their debts with cash that they did not have. To make matters worse, many of these farmers had served in the American Revolution with little or no pay and were unable to repay their debts when they returned.

In response, creditors began bringing the farmers to court, where they faced imprisonment and foreclosure of their property. With the reasoning that no court sessions meant no foreclosure, the farmers in western Massachusetts used the same prewar tactics and prevented the state courts from sitting.

The sentiment of many of these farmers was expressed in an interview published in the October 25, 1786 issue of the *Massachusetts Centinel*. The speaker, only identified as "an old plough jogger," told the writer:

> *I have laboured hard all my days, and fared hard. I have been greatly abused, been obliged to do more than my part in the war, been loaded with class-rates, town-rates, province-rates, continental-rates, and all rates, lawsuits, and have been pulled and hauled by sheriffs, constables and collectors, and had my cattle sold for less than they were worth. I have been obliged to pay and nobody will pay me. I have lost a great deal by this man, and that man, and t'other man, and the great men are going to get all we have, and I think it is time for us to rise and put a stop to it, and have no more courts, nor sheriffs, nor collectors, nor lawyers. I design to pay no more, and I know we have the biggest party, let them say what they will.*

In August 1786, a mob prevented the Court of Common Pleas from meeting in Northampton, and a month later, the Supreme Judicial Court arrived in Springfield to, among other things, put the leaders of the mob on trial. The Supreme Judicial Court was the highest court in the state, but the four justices were met at the Springfield courthouse by around one thousand men, led by Revolutionary War veterans Daniel Shays of Pelham and Luke Day of West Springfield.

About eight hundred soldiers in the state militia, under the command of General William Shepard, were present to counter the threat of the protestors, and from September 25 to 29, the two sides were engaged in a standoff in downtown Springfield. The court was open during this time, but there were no jurors available to serve, so Shepard abandoned the courthouse and dispersed his army.

The building was the scene of one other incident several months later, on December 26, when a group of about 350 men took the courthouse unopposed and prevented the Court of Common Pleas from convening.

The last major event in Shays' Rebellion came a month later, in January 1787, when Daniel Shays led an attack on the Springfield Arsenal, just up the hill from the courthouse. General Shepard was again there to meet them and ordered grapeshot to be fired into the crowd as it advanced. Four were killed, and the rest of Shays's army retreated with no further bloodshed.

The rebellion had largely collapsed after the defeat at the arsenal, but it proved to have lasting consequences in American history. At the time, the weak national government under the Articles of Confederation had been powerless to stop the rebellion, a point illustrated by the fact that the only national arsenal in the country had nearly been taken by a rebel force whose only opposition was a state militia. In part out of fear of anarchy brought on by Shays' Rebellion, the states convened in Philadelphia just a few months later to begin writing what would become the U.S. Constitution.

As for the courthouse that had been a focal point of the rebellion, it remained in use for only a few more years. By the 1790 census, Hampshire County had grown to nearly sixty thousand residents, and Springfield was just the sixth-largest town, behind more rural communities such as Granville and Conway. Northampton had also grown larger than Springfield, and in part because of its central location, the county seat was shifted there in 1794.

Following the court's departure, the old building was used as a town hall for some time, but county government soon returned to Springfield when the southern third of Hampshire County became Hampden County in 1812. Springfield was made the shire town, and for the next ten years, the old courthouse resumed its former role.

A new courthouse opened in 1822, and a few years later, the old building was sold to First Church for $800. In 1842, the South Church split off from the congregation, and the First Church gave it the old courthouse, which the church used for their services until a new building on Bliss Street was completed.

During its lifetime, the building was moved around a number of times, eventually ending up on the south side of Sanford Street, where the MassMutual Center is now located. It stood here as a carriage shop until about 1872, when it was dismantled and its timbers were used to build a tobacco barn.

## HAMPDEN COUNTY COURTHOUSE (1822)

Although Hampden County had been established in 1812, it took another ten years before its first permanent courthouse would be built. This was in part because of a dispute about the location; downtown businessmen and the leaders of the First Church wanted the courthouse to be built next to their meetinghouse, while the leaders of the new Unitarian congregation, including influential businessman Jonathan Dwight, wanted it built next to their church on State Street.

In this particular dispute, the distance was largely immaterial, as the two proposed locations were less than a quarter mile apart. There were certainly some financial interests involved, as both the Main Street businessmen and Jonathan Dwight were looking for the courthouse to increase their respective property values, but there was a symbolic nature to the argument as well. Main Street represented the town's traditional commercial and political center, and the First Church represented the traditional Congregational theology. State Street, on the other hand, represented the town's growth westward up the hill toward the new armory, and the Unitarian Church represented a new, liberal theology that was changing the nature of the church across New England at the time.

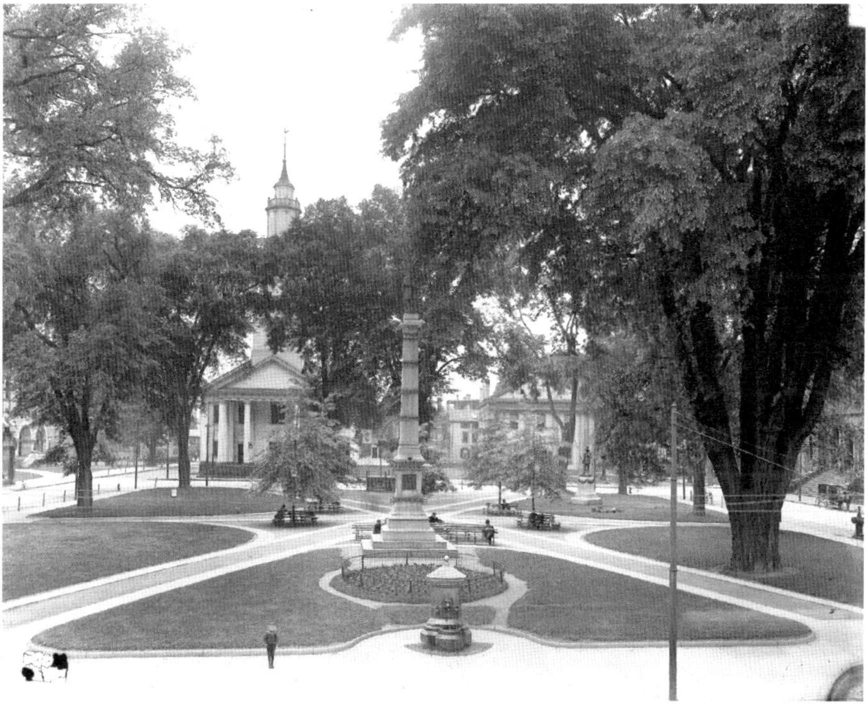

Court Square around 1905, with Old First Church on the left and the 1822 courthouse on the right. *Library of Congress.*

In the end, though, the business and religious interests along Main Street won out, and the new courthouse was built in 1822 on a lot directly adjacent to the First Church, fronting the recently developed Court Square. Like the church, it was designed by Isaac Damon. Because of this, there were plenty of similarities between the two buildings; the courthouse's Greek Revival style, with a triangular portico supported by four columns and a small cupola on top, matched the much larger church building. It was also virtually identical to Damon's Hampshire County Courthouse, which was completed the same year, in Northampton.

One of the most prominent trials in this courthouse was the murder trial of twelve-year-old Moses Elliot, who was accused of killing his friend, thirteen-year-old Josiah Buckland. In April 1834, Moses shot Josiah while the boys were firing at targets with their pistols. Moses then ran off, sold the pistol, acquired a spade to presumably bury the body and told Josiah's father that he had run away to Boston.

The next day, Josiah's brother found him, alive but badly wounded and delirious. He died four days later, after making a dying declaration that Moses had deliberately shot him. On the basis of this statement, along with Moses's suspicious activity after the incident and his general reputation as a mischievous boy, the twelve-year-old was charged with capital murder.

The trial, which was held in September, attracted significant attention, and not only was the courtroom full, but crowds gathered outside to listen. It was heard by the Supreme Judicial Court, with the state attorney general and the district attorney prosecuting. Defending Moses Elliot were Oliver B. Morris, who was the county judge of probate, and George Ashmun, a lawyer and state legislator who would later serve in Congress.

The defense argued that the shooting was accidental and called into question Josiah's mental state when he gave his account before dying. Although his mother testified that he had moments of lucidity, the doctors who cared for him described him as being insane after the shooting. The physical evidence, such as the location of his wound, also seemed to contradict the victim's story. As for Moses's actions after the shooting, such as disposing of the pistol and getting a spade, the defense argued that these were the result of his age and state of panic at the time. Ultimately, the jury agreed with the defense and, after two hours of deliberation, found Moses not guilty.

Murder trials were relatively uncommon in nineteenth-century Springfield, but there were several other cases at the old courthouse that garnered attention. Among these was the 1860 trial of Alexander

Desmarteau, a twenty-two-year-old French Canadian immigrant from Chicopee who was charged with raping seven-year-old Augustine Lucas, beating her to death and then throwing her body into the Connecticut River. He was tried under a new Massachusetts law that created different degrees of murder, and after being convicted of first-degree murder and sentenced to death, he appealed to the state Supreme Judicial Court, arguing that the law was unconstitutional. The court upheld his conviction, though, and he was executed in the county jail on State Street in 1861.

The last significant trial in the old courthouse was the 1873 murder trial of another twenty-two-year-old, Albert H. Smith of Westfield. Smith had worked as a switchman on the Boston & Albany Railroad, and in the summer of 1872, he met twenty-five-year-old Jennie Bates, who lived in her father's house near the railroad station in Westfield. The nature of their relationship was disputed at the trial, with Albert claiming that they had been intimately involved and were engaged to be married, while Bates claimed that they were merely acquaintances.

Regardless of what their relationship had been, by the fall of 1872, Jennie was engaged to another man, Charles D. Sackett, a fairly wealthy man who was about forty years old. On the night of November 20, Charles and Jennie watched a play together, and when he escorted her back to her father's house, Albert was waiting. He shot at them, hitting Jennie three times—one bullet struck her head. Charles was hit once, with the bullet puncturing his right lung. Jennie made a full recovery, and Charles appeared to be improving. But then infection set in. He died thirteen days later.

At the trial, Albert's lawyers used the insanity defense, arguing that his family history of mental illness, combined with his infatuation with Jennie, caused him to live under the delusion that they were actually married. Therefore, his state of mind when he killed Charles was not that of a spurned lover but rather as a jealous husband who wanted to protect his marriage. The defense had two doctors testify to his insanity at the time of the crime, and Albert's mother testified about the mental illness in her family and also produced a letter that he had written in September, telling her that he was married.

Newspaper accounts of the day indicate that the defense was particularly persuasive to many of the spectators at the trial, but ultimately, the jury voted to convict him of first-degree murder. He was sentenced to death, and shortly before his execution, he met with a reporter from the *Springfield Republican*. He showed the reporter an envelope with a lock of Jennie's hair in it and several photographs of her, including one that he planned to be buried with. Regarding his impending death, he remarked, "Why should I not want to die when all is taken from me? All that I prize on this earth is Jennie, and if she is taken, give me death."

Aside from murder trials, another notable event that was mentioned in several historic accounts of the courthouse occurred in August 1832, when about one hundred Revolutionary War veterans arrived at its doors. It was a very different scene from the one at the old courthouse nearly fifty years earlier, when hundreds of veterans had gathered during Shays' Rebellion. Instead of closing the courthouse, these men were there to file a pension claim under a new congressional act that awarded lifetime pensions at full pay for veterans with at least two years of service in the war and proportional pensions for those with fewer than two years but more than six months of service.

By then, over fifty years since the end of the war, most of the veterans would have been in their seventies or older, but nationwide, over fifteen thousand applied for pensions under the new act. The hundred or so who arrived at the Springfield courthouse that summer were the cause of a patriotic celebration, which included hanging a portrait of George Washington in the courthouse. It was painted from an original Gilbert Stuart portrait by local artist William S. Elwell and reportedly brought tears to the eyes of at least one veteran, who remarked, "Oh, yes, it looks like the old general."

As the county continued to grow in the mid-1800s, the courthouse became inadequate, and in 1851, it was expanded fifteen feet in the back, allowing larger offices for the clerk, register of deeds and register of probate. However, even this was not enough, and in 1869, a grand jury indicted the county commissioners for misconduct because they had not provided the courthouse with fireproof rooms to store important records.

Two years later, construction began on a new courthouse, and the old one closed in 1874. It was sold to the Independent Order of Odd Fellows, a fraternal organization that used the building as a lodge. The Odd Fellows remained there for about thirty years, until the building was demolished in 1906. The site is now part of Court Square, in between Old First Church and city hall along West Court Street.

## HAMPDEN COUNTY COURTHOUSE (1874)

The planning for the third Hampden County Courthouse began in 1871, when the county commissioners purchased land between State and Elm Streets, just south of the First Church. That same year, Henry Hobson

Richardson received the commission to design the building. It was one of his early works, and biographer and architectural historian Henry-Russell Hitchcock described it as "the building in which Richardson first found himself." It was built in an I-shape, with a 150-foot tower on the Elm Street side and three arches in front of the main entrance, and made of granite quarried from nearby Monson.

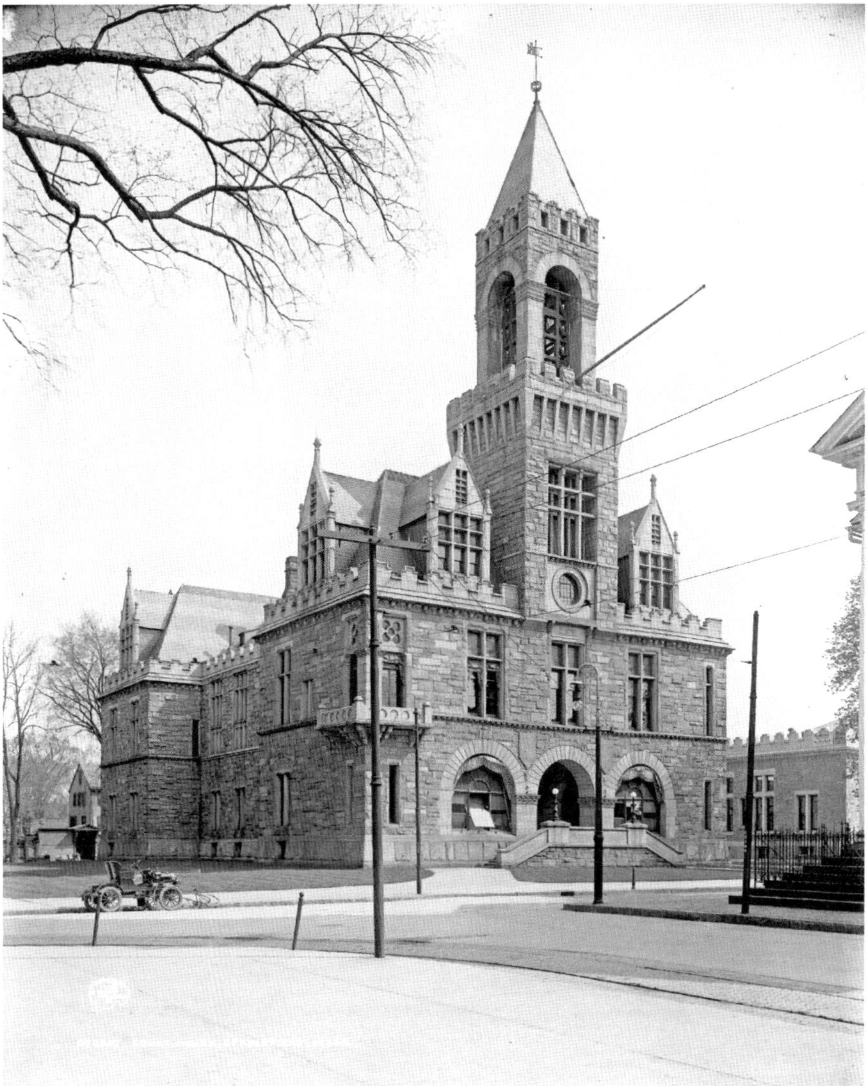

The Hampden County Courthouse in its original appearance, shortly before its 1906 remodeling. *Library of Congress.*

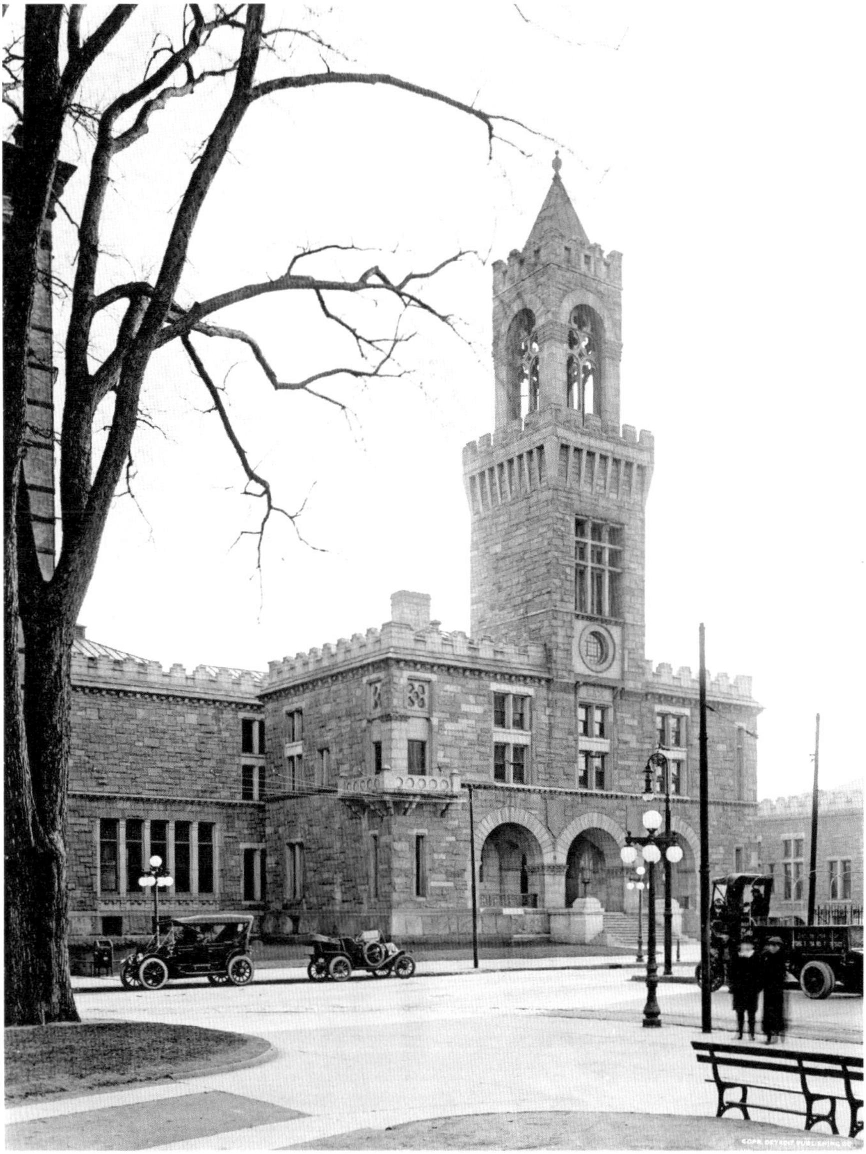

The Hampden County Courthouse around 1910–20, following the renovations that removed much of Richardson's original design. *Library of Congress.*

The courthouse opened on April 28, 1874, with an address by lawyer William G. Bates, who began his speech by describing the building as "a temple to the administration of the law." He then continued with a historical and philosophical examination of law, from the Old Testament and ancient

Rome to Shakespeare's *The Merchant of Venice*, before transitioning into a history of Springfield and Hampden County and then concluding with a long list of biographies of notable members of the county bar association.

The following day, the *Springfield Republican* approved of both Bates's speech and Richardson's architecture, describing the building's "massive reality of its granite arches, bent as a Roman would bend them, and the lofty spring of its Lombard tower" as being a contrast from their modern "age when veneering, imitation and hollowness characterize the works of men."

In the same article, the *Republican* was confident in the building's future, writing that Springfield "need have no fears that the architectural creation will pass out of usefulness." However, within three decades, the building was too small for the growing county, and in 1906, Richardson's successors at Shepley, Rutan & Coolidge were hired to remodel the building. The firm added a new wing to the east side of the courthouse, built a matching hall of records building just to the west and, most dramatically, removed the high roof and dormers on the third floor. This significantly altered the appearance of the building, and Hitchcock lamented that "it all but ruined the original qualities of the design."

With these changes, though, the building was able to see many more years of usefulness as the county courthouse. One of the more notable events in its history was an attempted bombing in 1934 by John Kaminski. A year earlier, John's brother Alexander had been serving a six-month sentence in Springfield's old York Street Jail for carrying a concealed weapon. He and fellow inmate Paul Wargo ambushed one of the guards, Merritt W. Hayden, and beat him with a two-by-four before stealing his keys. The pair escaped from the jail, and Hayden later died of a fractured skull. Wargo was quickly recaptured, but Kaminski made it as far as Lynchburg, Virginia, before being arrested for robbery, under an assumed name.

The two men were put on trial for murder, but on February 28, 1934, it was interrupted when John Kaminski entered the courtroom wearing a large overcoat. Sheriff David Manning recognized him, and as he approached him, Kaminski yelled that he had a bomb. He threw it at Manning. When it hit the floor, one of the percussion caps exploded, but it did not detonate the dynamite. Kaminski then pulled out a pistol, and as the two men struggled for it, Manning was shot in the thigh. The other officers in the courtroom then helped Manning subdue Kaminski without any further injuries.

The bomb's failure to detonate saved the lives of several dozen people who were in the courtroom, and it was carefully brought outside by police officers. After searching John Kaminski, they discovered that he was wearing steel plates as body armor and carrying two more explosive devices, a second gun, several knives and hundreds of rounds of ammunition. He was, in the words of the deputy sheriffs, a "walking arsenal."

Sheriff Manning recovered from his injuries and went on to serve Hampden County until the 1960s. John Kaminski was charged with attempted murder and later convicted, and in the meantime, his brother's murder trial continued as scheduled. The two were found guilty, and Wargo was sentenced to life in prison, while Alexander Kaminski was sentenced to death.

The drama did not end there, though. Prior to his sentencing, Alexander was returned to the York Street Jail and kept in his cell under increased security. Despite the law's best efforts, though, he escaped again on September 17, 1934, by sawing through the bottom of the bars in his cell and then bending them out of the way. This time, he remained at large for two months before being arrested at an Albany bus station. He was returned to Springfield for sentencing, and on February 19, 1935, he was executed in the electric chair at the Charlestown State Prison in Boston.

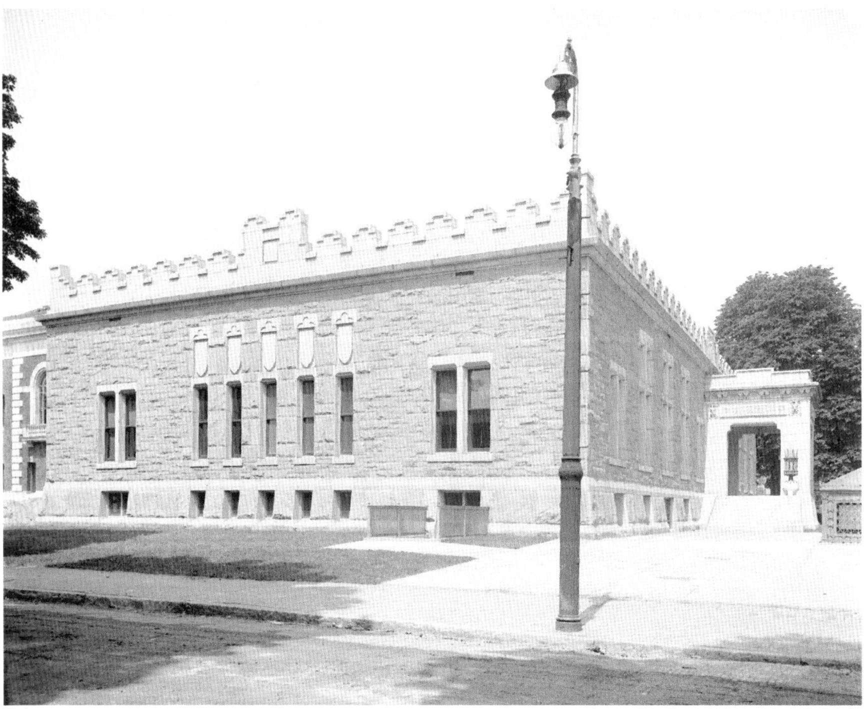

The hall of records building from State Street, around 1906–10. *Library of Congress.*

By the 1960s, there were plans to replace the nearly century-old courthouse with a new hall of justice that would consolidate the county government into a new, larger building. It took another decade before it opened in 1976, on the site where the hall of records had stood just to the west of the old courthouse. Architecturally, its boxy, concrete Brutalist design could not have contrasted more with Richardson's intricately designed Romanesque building, and it has not aged well, either. Less than forty years after it opened, there were already calls to replace it with a new courthouse, with proponents citing the building's malfunctioning elevators, poor heating and cooling systems and mold growth. In the meantime, though, the 1874 courthouse remains in use by the Housing Court and Juvenile Court, and despite the extensive alterations to Richardson's design, it remains one of the city's most prominent architectural landmarks.

## OLD CITY HALL

When Springfield became a city in 1852, its government was operating out of the old town hall on State Street. Although it had been built only twenty-four years earlier, this nondescript three-story brick structure was inadequate to house the new city government, and two years later, the cornerstone was laid for a new city hall. Located at the northwest corner of Court Square, it was right in the heart of the growing city, alongside other important buildings such as the county courthouse and the First Church.

The building was designed by prominent architect Leopold Eidlitz as an early example of the Romanesque Revival style that would, in the following decades, become predominant for public buildings in the United States. Its brick exterior was trimmed with brownstone from Longmeadow, and like the Romanesque architects that followed, Eidlitz made ample use of arches over the doors and windows. The building featured a 130-foot bell tower on the right side, and the interior had ample space for the mayor, city council and various city departments on the first floor, with a 2,300-seat auditorium on the upper floor. The basement housed the police department, including the city lockup, which was located directly underneath the tower.

It was dedicated on January 1, 1856, with a ceremony that the *Springfield Republican* described as having "the largest audience that ever found itself under one roof in this part of the state." Author and historian Josiah Gilbert Holland delivered an hour-long keynote speech at the ceremony. During his

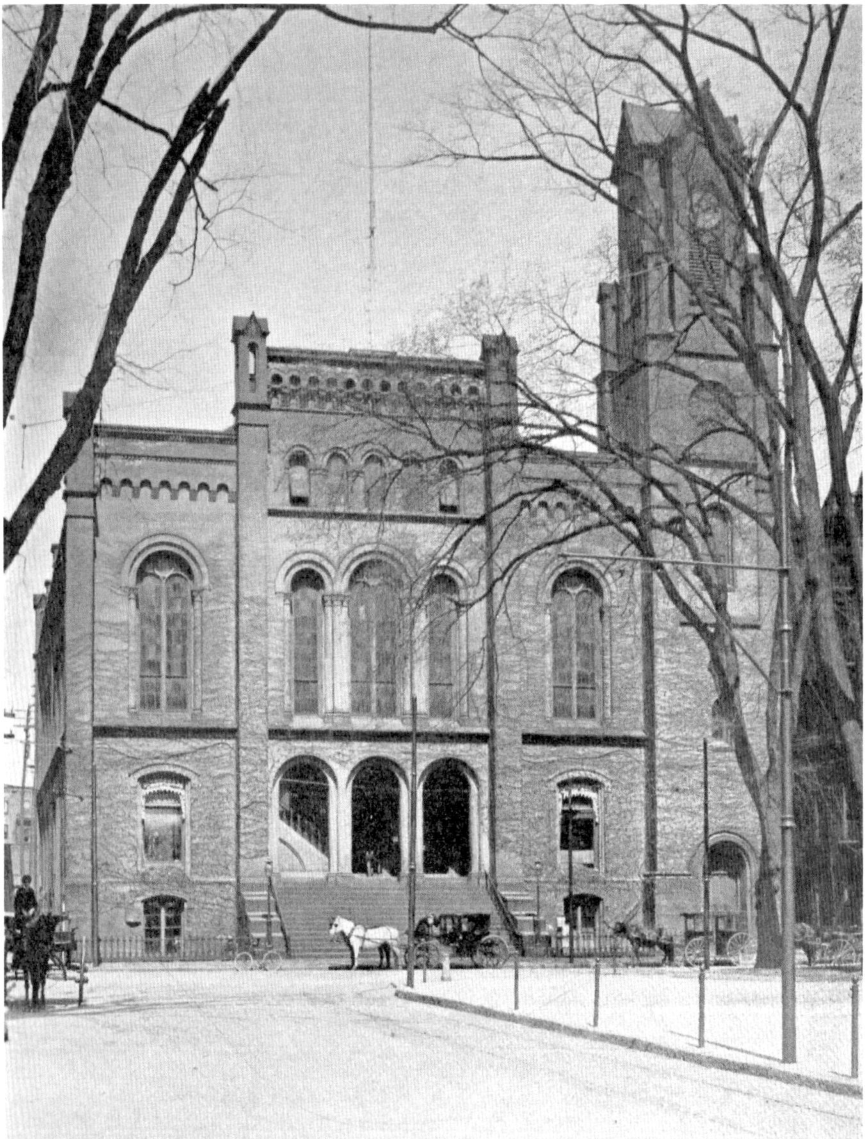

The old city hall, shortly before it burned down in 1905. *From* Springfield Present and Prospective, *1905.*

speech, he praised the building's architecture as a source of much-needed civic pride and as a "teacher of new and beautiful architectural ideas" in a city where "every public building is a failure, half a dozen of them are a disgrace, and two or three, unpardonable sins." He also took the time to chastise those who opposed public spending, expressing a hope that the success of the building would "break down individual selfishness and stinginess, and broaden the path for a larger public spirit."

The ceremony was followed a week later with a dedication ball, which included a twenty-piece orchestra, dancing and, perhaps most importantly, a "generous supply of refreshments." The proceeds from the two-dollar tickets went to the Springfield Association for the Relief of the Poor, and about one thousand guests attended. This number was much lower than expected, but the *Republican* described it as "a beautiful, brilliant assembly. There were just enough present to make it pleasant, without an immense crowd. The floor was always full, and a more beautiful collection of well dressed ladies rarely find themselves together."

During its time as city hall, this building saw Springfield's population grow from about twelve thousand in the 1850s to over sixty-two thousand by the turn of the century, and it probably could have remained in use for much longer had it not been destroyed in perhaps the most bizarre disaster in the city's history. On January 6, 1905, the second-floor hall was being used for a two-week-long food fair when a fire started. It was believed to have been caused when a monkey at one of the exhibits in the fair knocked over a kerosene lamp. Once ignited, the fire spread quickly throughout the building, aided by the fair's flammable decorations and the building's dry timbers.

The fire started at about 12:50 p.m., when most of the city hall workers on the first floor were on their lunch breaks. About a dozen were still in the building, and they remained as long as they could, not realizing how fast the flames were moving above their heads. Just seven minutes after the fire started, the roof began to collapse, but the workers managed to save the city records by moving them into vaults or by breaking windows and throwing them onto the snowbanks outside.

There were no lives lost in the fire—even the monkey survived—but several of the city employees had close calls, including city clerk assistant Bertha Fuller, who moved books and papers into the vault even after the ceiling started collapsing. She ended up trapped and had to be rescued, with fire raining down from the ceiling as they escaped the building. Aside from smoke inhalation and a few singed hairs, though, she was not seriously injured.

City hall was a total loss, and since it was uninsured, the city bore the whole cost of replacing it. The neighboring buildings were also damaged by the fire, but overall, it could have been much worse. During the fire, the wind was blowing from the east, away from Main Street. The fire department worked tirelessly to contain the fire, but had the winds been blowing in the

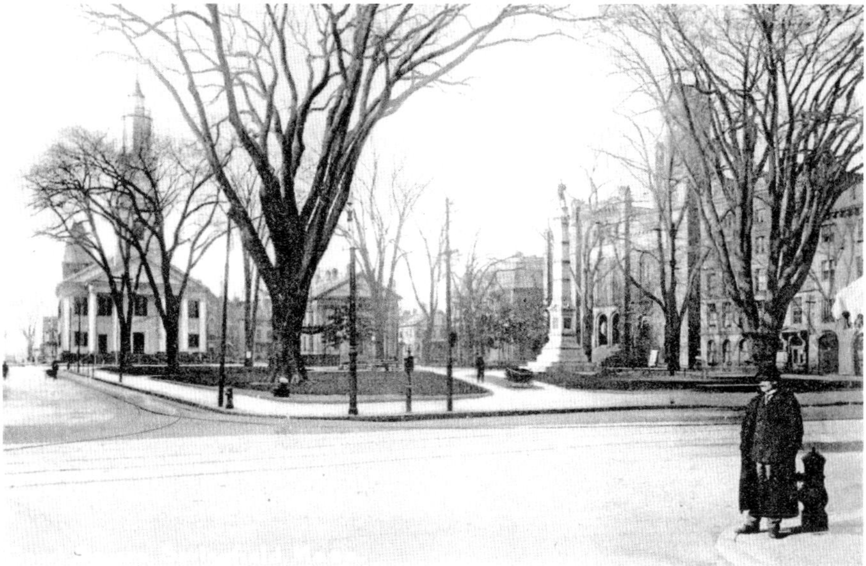

Early twentieth-century postcard view of Court Square, showing the old courthouse in the center and the old city hall on the right. *Author's collection.*

opposite direction the firefighters might not have been able to prevent it from spreading and engulfing much of downtown Springfield.

Ultimately, the fire provided the city with the opportunity to build the Springfield Municipal Group, which was completed in 1913. It includes city hall, which was built on the same site as the old one, plus the matching Symphony Hall and the three-hundred-foot campanile tower in the middle. The only reminder left of the old building is the bell, which is located next to the steps of city hall in about the same spot where its tower once stood. Although badly cracked, the two-ton bell still has the date of the building's dedication, the misspelled name of "Springfild" and a strangely appropriate Latin inscription that translates to "Behold, O man! I proclaim the hours. So passes the glory of life. When the fire rages I summon the people."

## Old Post Office

Springfield's first post office was established in 1775 with Moses Church as the postmaster. At the time, there was no dedicated building for the post office, so Church operated it out of his hat and fur shop on the northeast corner of Main and Court Streets. For the next century, the post office moved around to nine other locations around Court Square until 1891, when it finally received a building of its own.

Built on the west side of Main Street between Worthington and Fort Streets, it was the first purpose-built post office building in the city. Its architect was William A. Freret, who designed a number of post offices and other federal buildings across the country in his capacity as the head of the Office of the Supervising Architect from 1887 to 1888. Freret's design reflects the popular Romanesque style of the era, and like many other public buildings in Springfield, it was constructed with Longmeadow brownstone.

Prior to construction, the *Springfield Republican* published the plans for the building in January 1888. The paper approved of the design, describing it as "picturesque and even striking," with characteristics of "strength and dignity." The following day, the newspaper reported that the plans were well received by the public, with the only criticism being the eight steps up to the main entrance, which people argued would be inconvenient and

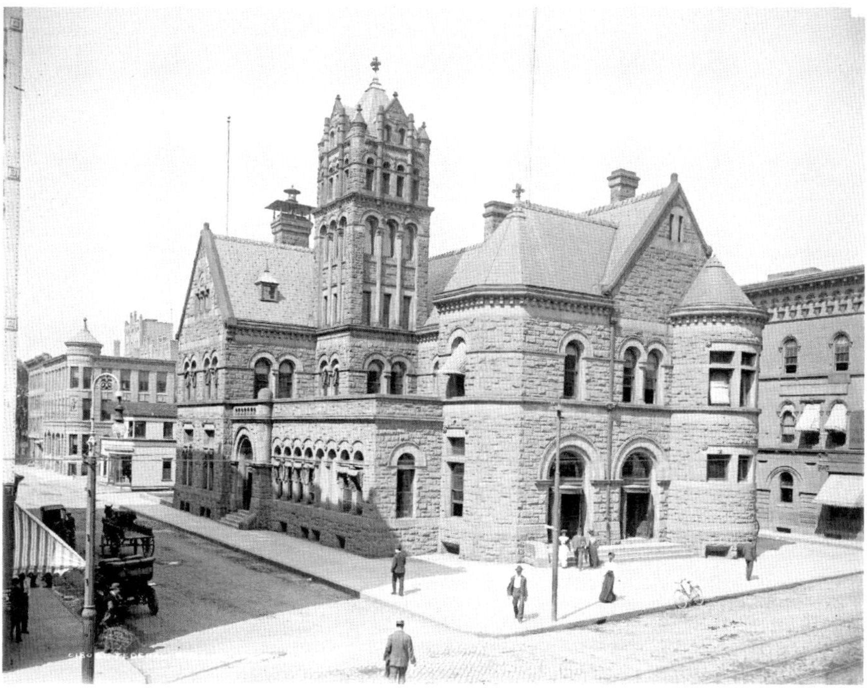

The old post office building, seen from the corner of Main and Worthington Streets around 1905. *Library of Congress.*

possibly dangerous, especially in the winter. Freret apparently listened to their concerns because the finished building had just four steps up to the main entrance.

The two-story building housed the post office on the first floor, with customs and other federal offices on the second floor, but it did not take long to outgrow the space. By the early twentieth century, it was expanded in the back, and branch offices were established around Springfield. But even this was not enough to meet the demands of the growing city. It was replaced in 1932 by a new building on Dwight Street, which included a post office and a federal courtroom, as well as office space for everyone from the U.S. attorney and customs to the Prohibition administrator.

Part of the construction of the new post office involved creating a new street behind it, which was named in honor of W. Kirk Kaynor, probably the most notable postmaster to serve in the old 1891 post office. He was appointed postmaster by Warren Harding in 1923 and remained in the position until 1928, when he was elected to the U.S. House of Representatives. Kaynor served in Congress for less than a year, though, before he was killed in a plane crash in Washington, D.C., on December 20, 1929. It was his first time in an airplane. He was planning on flying back to Springfield to surprise his family for Christmas, but the plane crashed less than a minute after takeoff, killing all five people on board.

The old post office building was demolished in 1933, just forty-two years after it opened. The site was briefly occupied by a bus terminal, and then in 1939, the Enterprise department store was built here. It is still standing, but its bland Art Deco design hardly compares to the "strength and dignity" of the old Romanesque post office that it replaced.

# 4 INDUSTRY

Much of Springfield's nineteenth-century growth and economic prosperity was due to its industries, but it was very different from other New England factory cities that developed after the Industrial Revolution. Springfield's location may have been ideal for transportation, but it was not particularly well suited for industry. The slow-moving Connecticut River barely drops in elevation in the city, and the Mill River was too small for large-scale industrial use. Chicopee, which was originally part of Springfield, had factories along the Chicopee River, but it became a separate town in 1848. The only part of the river left in Springfield was in the northeastern corner of the city at Indian Orchard, over five miles from downtown.

As a result of its geography, Springfield never developed large-scale industrial complexes like the paper mills of Holyoke or the textile mills of Lowell and Fall River, but in the long run, this proved to be a benefit. While these cities were almost entirely dependent on their respective industries, Springfield had a much more diversified economy. By the early twentieth century, the city was producing goods such as board games, ice skates, automobiles, railroad cars, motorcycles, candy, beer and, of course, its best-known product, firearms.

# Springfield Armory

Of all the industries in Springfield, none was as instrumental in bringing prosperity as the Springfield Armory, whose roots trace back to the American Revolution. In the fall of 1776, Colonel Henry Knox recommended to Congress that the army should have "capital Laboratories erected at a distance from the seat of war" to use as arsenals. George Washington agreed and suggested that one should be located at Hartford, but Congress preferred Brookfield, Massachusetts. Knox, though, had passed through Springfield during the previous winter while bringing cannons from Fort Ticonderoga to Boston, and he believed that it would be the ideal location for such an arsenal. It was on the east–west road from Boston to Albany and had access to water transportation on the Connecticut River, yet it was also upstream from the rapids near Windsor, which prevented oceangoing ships from attacking the town. Because of this, Knox wrote, "[T]he plain just above Springfield is perhaps one of the most proper Spots in America on every Account." Congress ultimately followed his recommendation, establishing the arsenal in Springfield in 1777.

During the war, the facility was primarily used for storing and repairing weapons and making cartridges. It served well in this role, and Knox's choice in location proved to be wise because the arsenal was never threatened by British soldiers. The only serious threat came several years after the war ended, during Shays' Rebellion. By this point, its manufacturing role had ended, and the arsenal was just used for storing weapons, such as muskets and powder. Enticed by this cache, Daniel Shays led a large force that attempted to take the arsenal in January 1787. In the climactic event of Shays' Rebellion, the arsenal was successfully defended, and the valuable supplies were secure.

The role of the arsenal changed again in 1794, when Congress authorized two national armories to manufacture firearms for the army and state militias. President Washington selected Harpers Ferry, Virginia, for one of the armories, and Springfield was a logical choice for the other one since it already had the existing facilities along with a proven record from the war. The only limitation at the Springfield site was water power, so part of the development of the armory included building shops along the Mill River, about a mile from the main site on State Street.

None of the eighteenth-century buildings are still standing at the armory. The oldest one left is the West Arsenal, which was completed in 1808 during the armory's first major building project. This expansion came just in time for the War of 1812, but even then, the armory had difficulty keeping up with demand. It produced about twelve thousand muskets per year during the war but spent even more time repairing older, defective guns.

After the war, the armory began making efforts to upgrade its production, including hiring inventor Thomas Blanchard, who developed a lathe for carving gunstocks. These gunstocks had previously been carved by hand, but the lathe did much of this time-consuming work and also produced identical gunstocks, marking a major advancement in the development of interchangeable parts.

Improvements continued under Major James Ripley, who became superintendent in 1842. At this point, many of the present-day buildings along the south and east sides of the green had already been built, but he added more buildings, with the most prominent being the Main Arsenal. Completed in 1850 on the west side of the green, it could store 300,000 guns, and the imposing three-story brick building with its tower became a defining feature of both the armory and the city.

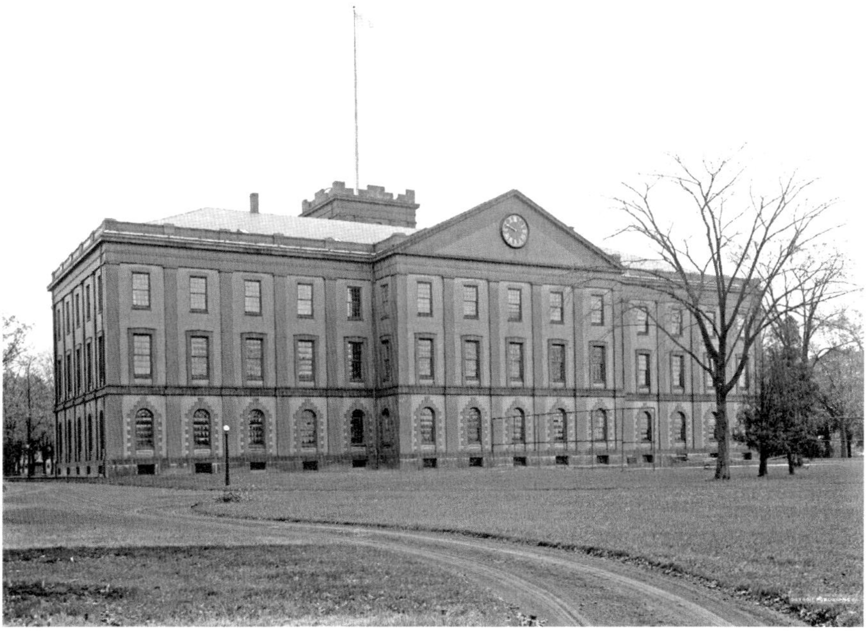

The Main Arsenal at the armory, around 1910–20. *Library of Congress.*

With these new buildings and production methods, the armory was producing over 20,000 guns per year by 1850, but it would soon dramatically increase its output with the start of the Civil War. In 1861, right at the beginning of the war, the Harpers Ferry Armory was destroyed to prevent capture by the Confederates, leaving Springfield as the only federal armory for the rest of the nineteenth century. The armory responded to the challenge, increasing its workforce from 200 to over 2,600 and making more than 276,000 guns per year by 1864. By the end of the war, it had produced over 800,000 rifles for the Union army, which was more than it had made in the previous sixty-six years combined.

As devastating as the Civil War was for the country as a whole, it brought significant growth to Springfield. Along with over two thousand new jobs at the armory, other firearms manufacturers in the area increased their workforces, bringing large numbers of skilled laborers to the city. From 1860 to 1865, the population of Massachusetts had largely stagnated, but Springfield grew by 45 percent.

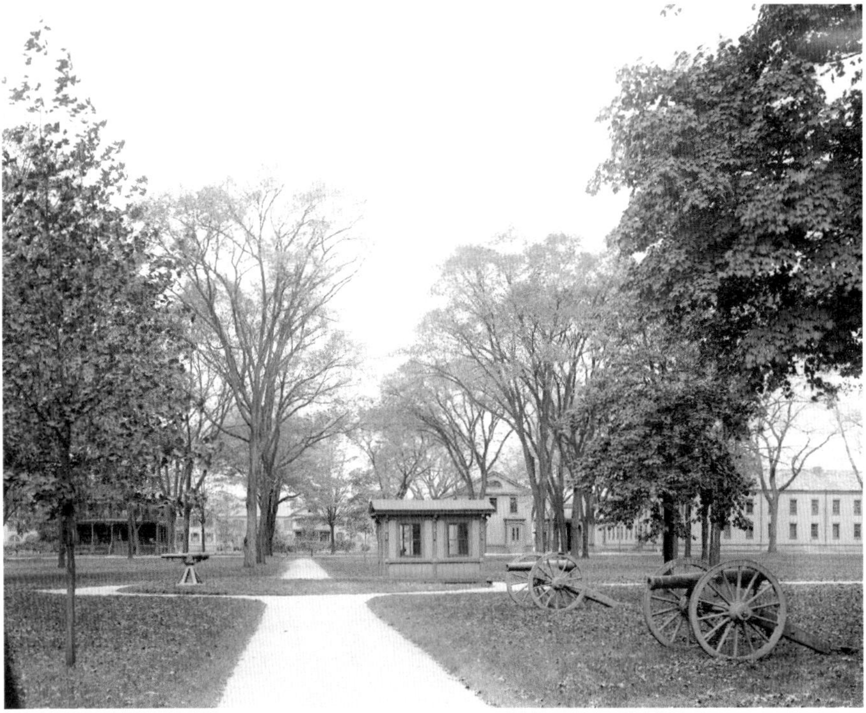

The armory grounds, facing north from the center of the green toward Officers' Row, around 1910–20. *Library of Congress.*

After the war, Springfield's population continued to increase, as did the armory's importance to the nation's military. No longer just a place to produce and store weapons, it took on another role in developing new firearms. One of the most significant was the M1903 rifle, which was developed here and became a mainstay in the U.S. military throughout the first half of the twentieth century, including during World War I and World War II. It was followed in 1936 by the M1 Garand, another Springfield creation that was developed here by civilian employee John Garand. It was the first standard-issue semiautomatic rifle in the world, and it was ready for production just in time for World War II, giving the United States a significant advantage. General George S. Patton described it as "the greatest battle implement ever devised," and the Springfield Armory produced around three and a half million during the war, operating twenty-four hours a day to keep up with demand.

After the war, the armory shifted almost exclusively to development, with production being outsourced to private contractors. During this

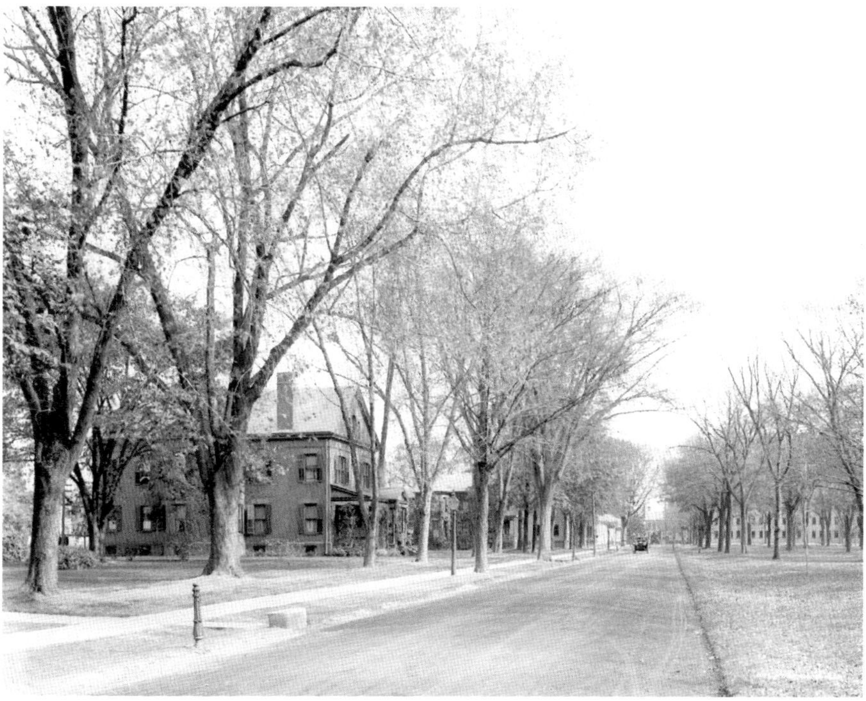

Officers' Row, facing east along the north side of the green at the armory, around 1910–20. *Library of Congress.*

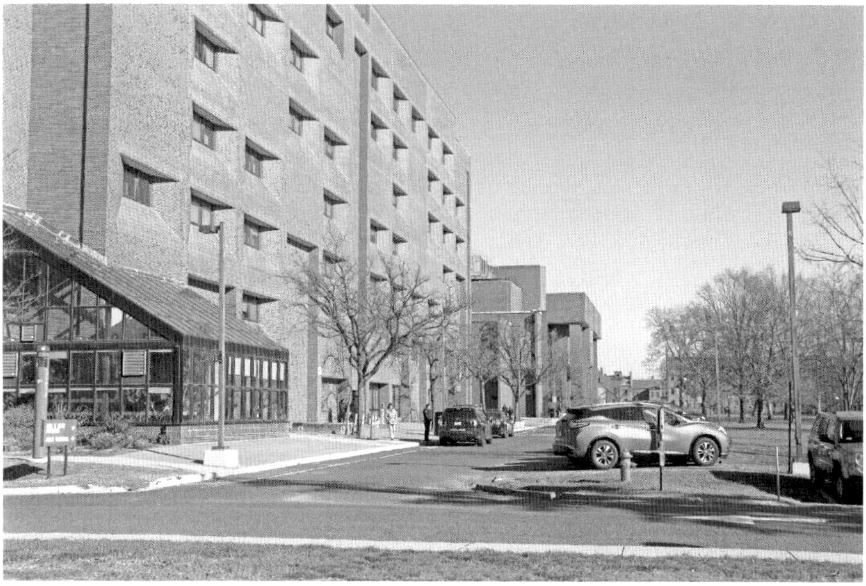

Modern classroom buildings at Springfield Technical Community College, where the Officers' Row houses once stood. *Author's collection.*

time, the M14 rifle was developed here along with other weapons, but the Department of Defense closed the facility in 1968, taking with it nearly 2,500 jobs and further hurting a city that was already experiencing economic difficulty and population loss.

The armory is now administered by the National Park Service as the Springfield Armory National Historic Site, and the Main Arsenal is now a museum, housing a large collection of antique firearms. Most of the other buildings have been converted into classrooms and offices for Springfield Technical Community College, but some of the historic buildings have been lost since the armory closed. The north side of the green was once known as Officers' Row, with four houses that were used by the officers who were stationed here. The oldest dated back to the 1830s, but they were demolished in the early 1970s to build three large classroom buildings that now stand on the site. Otherwise, the rest of the armory has been preserved, and it remains an important reminder of the role that Springfield has played in American history.

# SMITH & WESSON

Among the many workers whom the armory drew to Springfield was Silas Smith, who moved here from Cheshire, Massachusetts, around 1812 and began working at the armory's Watershops. With him was his four-year-old son Horace, who apprenticed as a bayonet forger in the armory after he turned sixteen. This began a lifelong career in the gun-making industry for Horace, who worked at the armory for eighteen years. In 1842, he began working for several different private gun manufacturers in New England, eventually meeting Daniel B. Wesson.

Nearly seventeen years younger than Smith, Wesson had apprenticed with his brother Edwin, where he learned to make guns and worked in his firm until Edwin's death in 1849. The two men formed their first partnership in 1852 in Norwich, Connecticut. They sold the company to Oliver Winchester several years later, but in 1856, they formed a new Smith & Wesson company in Springfield and began selling their pistols the following year.

Prior to 1857, Samuel Colt's company in Hartford held a patent on revolvers, but with the expiration of the patent, Smith & Wesson was able to introduce its own improved version of the firearm. Colt's revolvers were front loading, requiring the user to individually add the powder, bullet and primer to each chamber in the cylinder. Smith & Wesson removed this time-consuming task by creating the first successful cartridge revolver. Along with

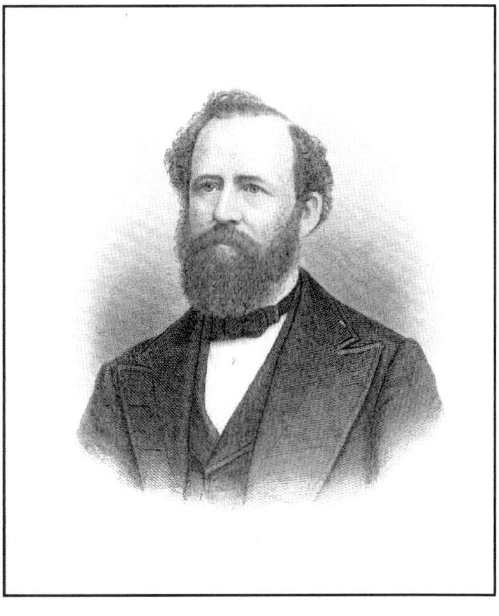

Engraving of Daniel B. Wesson. *From* King's Handbook of Springfield, *1884*.

creating a self-contained cartridge, it also purchased a patent from former Colt employee Rollin White, whose invention of a bored-through cylinder was the only practical way of designing such a revolver.

Because the patent gave Smith & Wesson a virtual monopoly over cartridge revolvers, it soon outgrew its modest facilities in a rented shop on Market Street. In 1859, it opened a new factory a few blocks away on Stockbridge Street. It was fortuitous timing, because the Civil War began just two years later. The company never received any military contracts during the war because its small-caliber .22 revolvers had little practical value in combat, but the bulk of its orders came from soldiers who wanted a personal sidearm to carry for protection. Their wartime production increased to an average of 2,500 revolvers per month, but like the armory up the hill, it still had trouble keeping up with the demand.

By the end of the war, their company was less than ten years old, but the two owners were already well on their way to accumulating substantial fortunes. Congress had passed an income tax during the war, and in 1866,

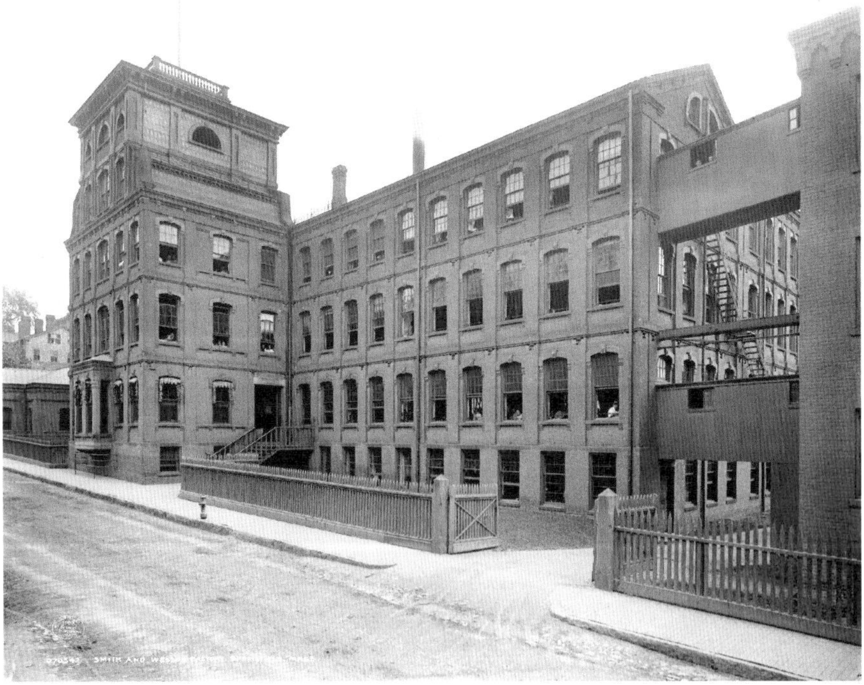

The original 1859 Smith & Wesson factory on Stockbridge Street, around 1908. *Library of Congress.*

the *Springfield Republican* published the names of over eight hundred residents along with their incomes from the previous year. Only those who made over $600 were on the list, and together they had a median income of just over $1,200. Of these, eleven earned over $20,000, including railroad and bank executive Chester W. Chapin, whose $78,880 income was the third highest in the city. However, Horace Smith and Daniel Wesson were in a class by themselves, earning $163,012 and $162,552, respectively.

The company continued developing new revolvers, including the .44-caliber Model 3, which it marketed toward military use. Customers included the U.S. Army, but it also became popular overseas, and in the 1870s, the Russian government alone purchased over 150,000 revolvers.

Horace Smith retired in 1873, selling his share of the company to Wesson. He spent the remaining twenty years of his life as a philanthropist and was described in the *Springfield Republican* after his death in 1893 as "the most liberal public benefactor that Springfield has ever seen." In his will, he left nearly all of his estimated $500,000 estate to a wide range of charities, including the City Library, Springfield Hospital, the Home for Friendless Women, the YMCA, Wesleyan Academy in Wilbraham and Booker T. Washington's Tuskegee College in Alabama.

In the meantime, Daniel Wesson continued to expand the company. By the 1880s, the facility had grown to fill much of the block between Stockbridge, Willow and Cross Streets, and around five hundred employees worked here, including Wesson's sons Walter and Joseph. They continued to innovate, and in 1899 Smith & Wesson introduced the Model 10, a .38-caliber revolver that became one of its most successful guns. It is still in production, with over six million sold after more than a century.

After Daniel Wesson's death in 1906, his sons took over the company, and it remained under the control of the Wesson family well into the twentieth century. Like the Springfield Armory, its factory was busy during World War II, and Smith & Wesson produced over one million revolvers for the U.S. military and its allies by the end of the war. At this point, though, the old buildings were obsolete, and like many other companies in the mid-twentieth century, it moved out of downtown Springfield. However, Smith & Wesson remained in the city, building a new facility in East Springfield on Roosevelt Avenue.

The fifteen factory buildings on Stockbridge Street were sold in 1951, and most have since been demolished, including the original 1859 factory, which once stood on the south side of the street just east of Willow Street. However, while the historic buildings are gone, Smith & Wesson is still headquartered in Springfield, and over 160 years after Horace Smith and Daniel Wesson first opened their revolver factory on Market Street, it remains one of the city's most recognizable corporations.

## WASON MANUFACTURING COMPANY

When *King's Handbook of Springfield* was published in 1884, it included a chapter with short descriptions of the various businesses in the city. The order in which they were listed gives some indication of how important they were considered, and Smith & Wesson appears second in the chapter. The first, however, was Wason Manufacturing Company, with the book explaining that "no manufactory in Springfield has become more world-famed; and none has, during the past twenty years, handled so much money."

Like so many of Springfield's successful nineteenth-century entrepreneurs, Thomas Wason came from humble beginnings. He was the son of a carpenter in Hancock, New Hampshire, and one of fifteen children. When they were young, he and his brother Charles worked alongside their father in his shop, where they learned skills that became valuable as adults, when they moved to Massachusetts.

In 1845, the brothers started their own business in Springfield, making railroad cars out of a shed that was too small to fit the entire car. As was the case with Smith & Wesson, their timing was perfect. They were honing their skills as railroad car manufacturers just as railroads were starting to spread across the country. Just a year later, they opened a larger facility on Liberty Street, and in 1848, they purchased the Springfield Car and Engine Company and moved into its buildings on Lyman Street.

Their new location was right next to the Boston & Albany Railroad yard, in the block between Lyman and Taylor Streets, on the west side of Dwight Street. Charles sold his share of the company to his brother in 1851 and moved to Cleveland, where he opened his own car manufacturing company. Thomas continued the business here in Springfield, building cars for nearly every major American railroad, including the country's first sleeping car, which was produced here in 1857. He even obtained foreign contracts, such as a 161-car order that was shipped to Egypt in 1860. Along with Springfield's other manufacturers, Wason's factory also contributed to the war effort during the Civil War, manufacturing gun carriages alongside its railroad cars.

Thomas Wason died in 1870 at the age of fifty-eight, and George C. Fisk took over as company president. Like Wason, Fisk was a New Hampshire native who came to Springfield in search of work, and in 1852, Wason hired him as a bookkeeper for one dollar per day. Fisk soon rose up the ranks, purchasing a one-sixth interest in the company in 1854 and later serving as treasurer and then vice-president.

Under Fisk's leadership, the Wason Manufacturing Company soon moved to a new, more spacious location outside of downtown, just south of the Chicopee line in the Brightwood neighborhood. It opened in 1872 on Wason Avenue, on the west side of the railroad tracks, and it included shops for every step in building a car, from a foundry to make the wheels to a paint shop for putting the finishing touches on the cars. The property included a twelve-acre lumberyard that could store up to four million feet of lumber, a necessity given that by the 1880s the facility was using thirty-five thousand feet per day. With over seven hundred workers, Wason was one of the largest employers in the city, and with around one hundred cars produced each day, it was the largest railroad car manufacturer in New England.

By the turn of the century, the company shifted its focus to making trolleys and rapid transit cars, including trolleys for the Springfield Street Railway and some of the first subway cars for New York City. In 1907, Wason was

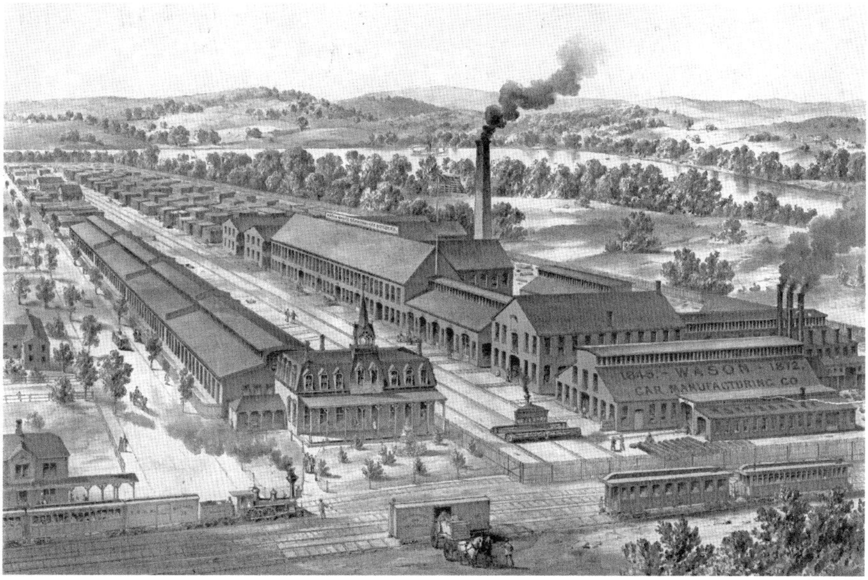


A print of the Wason Manufacturing Company facility in Brightwood, facing west toward the Connecticut River, around 1872. *Library of Congress.*

purchased by the Philadelphia-based J.G. Brill Company, and George Fisk retired after fifty-four years with the company. Wason became a subsidiary of Brill, which continued to operate the Springfield plant. However, by the early 1930s, the country was in the middle of the Great Depression, and buses were steadily replacing trolleys for public transportation, so in 1932, Brill closed the former Wason facility.

Over the next seventy-five years, the property changed hands several times, and most of the original 1870s buildings were demolished, leaving only the machine shop and foundry buildings. For many years, the site was owned by the Moore Drop Forging Company, and most recently, it was home to the Danaher Tool Company until it closed in 2005. All of the industrial buildings on the property, including the two surviving Wason buildings, were demolished soon after and replaced with medical office buildings.

## KIBBE BROTHERS COMPANY

Along with entrepreneurs like Horace Smith, Thomas Wason and George Fisk, nineteenth-century Springfield saw many other rags-to-riches stories, with young men coming to the city from rural communities and starting successful businesses. Two such men were brothers George and Horace Kibbe, who grew up on a farm in Somers, Connecticut. Their father died when they were young, and they spent most of their childhood working on the family farm. When Horace was seventeen, he took a job as a clerk in Longmeadow, but at his mother's insistence, he learned a trade and became a mason.

He much preferred business over masonry work, though, and in 1842, the twenty-two-year-old began working in Springfield for candy manufacturer Cicero Simons. Just a year later, Horace became a partner in the company, which was renamed Simons & Kibbe. His brother George later joined, and by the 1860s, it was renamed Kibbe Brothers & Company.

The original factory was located on Cross Street, but it later moved to the corner of Market and Sanford Streets and then, in 1862, to the Union Block at the southeast corner of Main Street and Harrison Avenue. At first, the focus of the company was on retail candy sales, but as the business grew, it shifted to wholesale production and distribution.

One of the distinctive features of the company was its distribution system. Although railroads connected Springfield to nearly every major city and town in New England, the Kibbes preferred horse-drawn wagons. At its peak, it had eight wagons, each pulled by four horses, that distributed candy to retailers on designated routes, traveling up to one hundred miles from Springfield. It proved to be a successful business model: each wagon made about one trip per month, leaving Springfield with around two tons of candy, and aside from delivering the candy, the vehicles had significant advertising value and were instantly recognizable in the towns on their routes.

George Kibbe died in 1882 and Horace in 1887, but the company continued under the Kibbe Brothers name. The new owners did make some changes, though. The long tradition of wagon distribution ended in 1888, and a few years later, the company moved into a new factory around the corner, on the south side of Harrison Avenue.

By 1910, Kibbe was producing about seventeen tons of candy per day, with a workforce of around 350. Many of these workers were children, and this drew the attention of prominent photographer and social reformer Lewis W. Hine. From 1906 to 1917, Hine worked for the National Child Labor Committee, traveling around the country and using his camera to document working conditions of young children in the days before strict

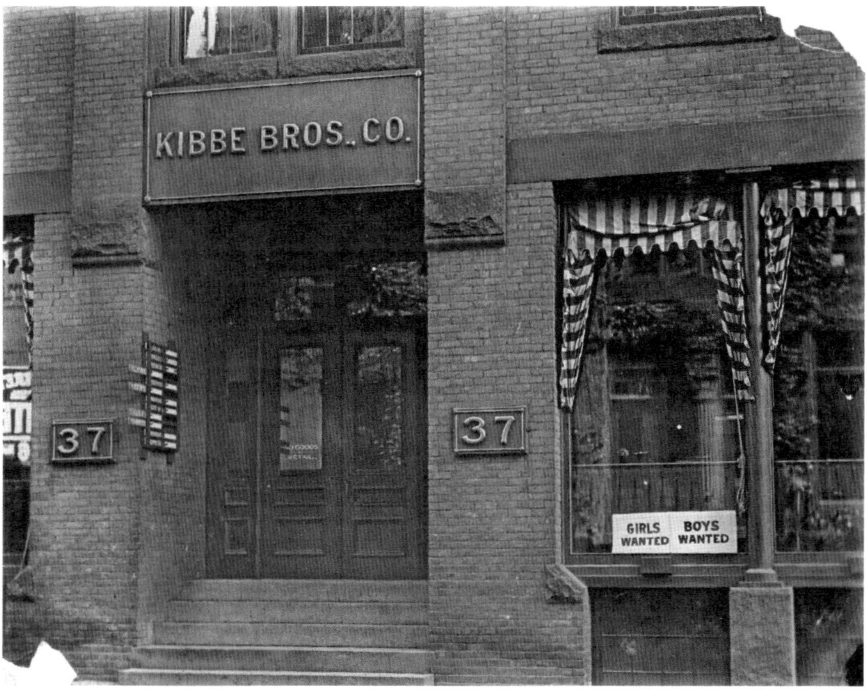


"Help Wanted" signs in the window at the Kibbe factory at 37 Harrison Avenue. Photographed by Lewis Hine in 1910. *Library of Congress.*

child labor laws. During this time, he made several visits to Springfield, including one in October 1910, when he photographed young workers at the Kibbe factory. According to his captions, their ages ranged from fourteen to sixteen, and they earned between $3.50 and $4.00 per week working as coconut shavers and chocolate machine operators.

Hine's work in Springfield and elsewhere helped to bring change, and in 1913, Massachusetts passed laws restricting the types of work that children could do, especially in potentially dangerous industrial jobs. Work at the Kibbe factory was not nearly as dangerous as some of the other places that Hine documented, but accidents still did happen. The factory used ammonia as a refrigerant to keep the chocolate rooms cool, and in one incident in April 1912, the gas line began leaking, filling the building with ammonia. Over one hundred workers, mostly young girls, were evacuated. They waited outside on Harrison Avenue, choking and coughing from the fumes, until the factory engineer found a gas mask and entered the basement to close the valve on the leaking pipe. No injuries were reported, and the girls returned to work once the fumes had been cleared from the building.

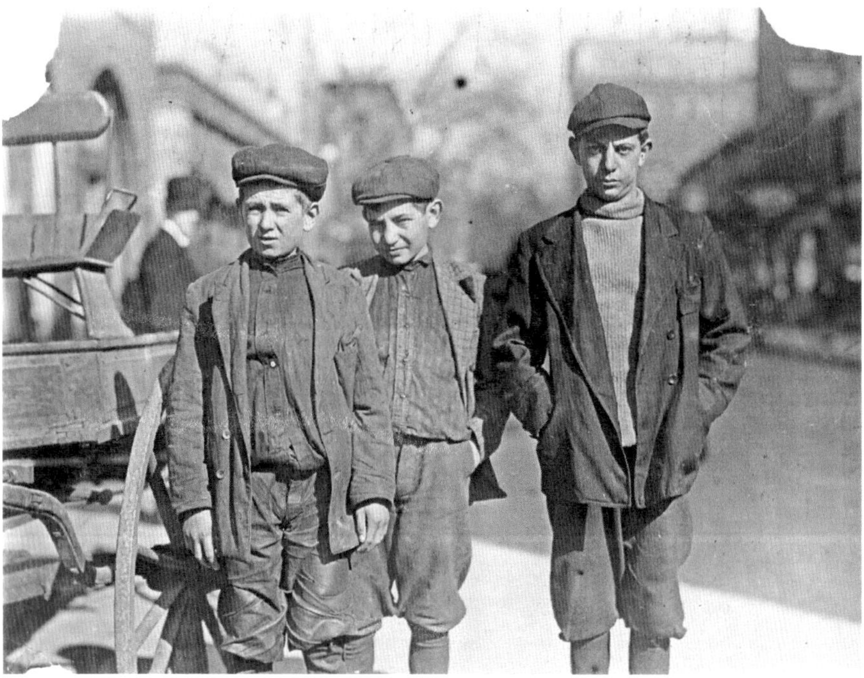

Kibbe workers Isaac and Jacob Futterman and William Cohan, who were between fifteen and sixteen years old at the time. Photographed by Lewis Hine in 1910. *Library of Congress.*

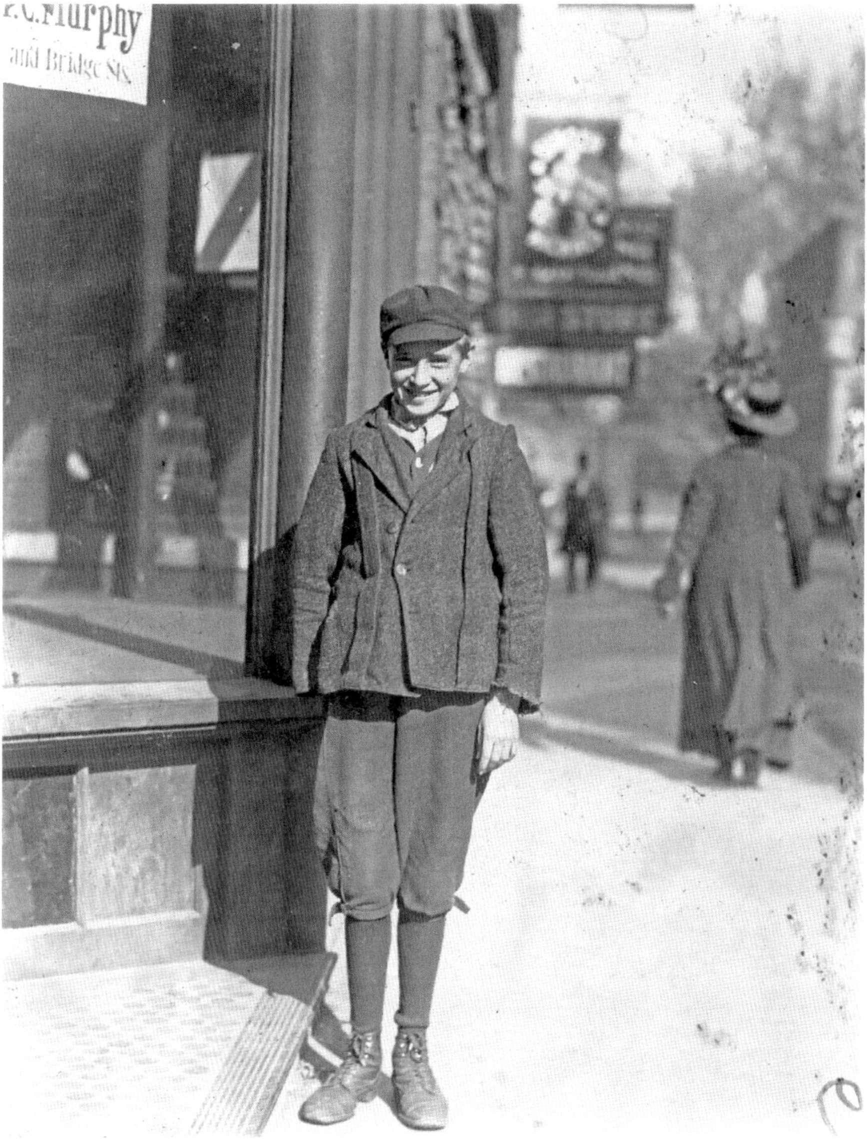

Fifteen-year-old Kibbe employee Earl Roberts, who earned four dollars per week operating a chocolate machine. Photographed by Lewis Hine in 1910. *Library of Congress.*

The company continued to grow into the 1920s. In a 1926 *Springfield Republican* article, the newspaper wrote that "the demand for candy is greater than ever," and by this point Kibbe had seven buildings in its Harrison Avenue facility, with around five hundred employees. They produced up to two hundred tons of

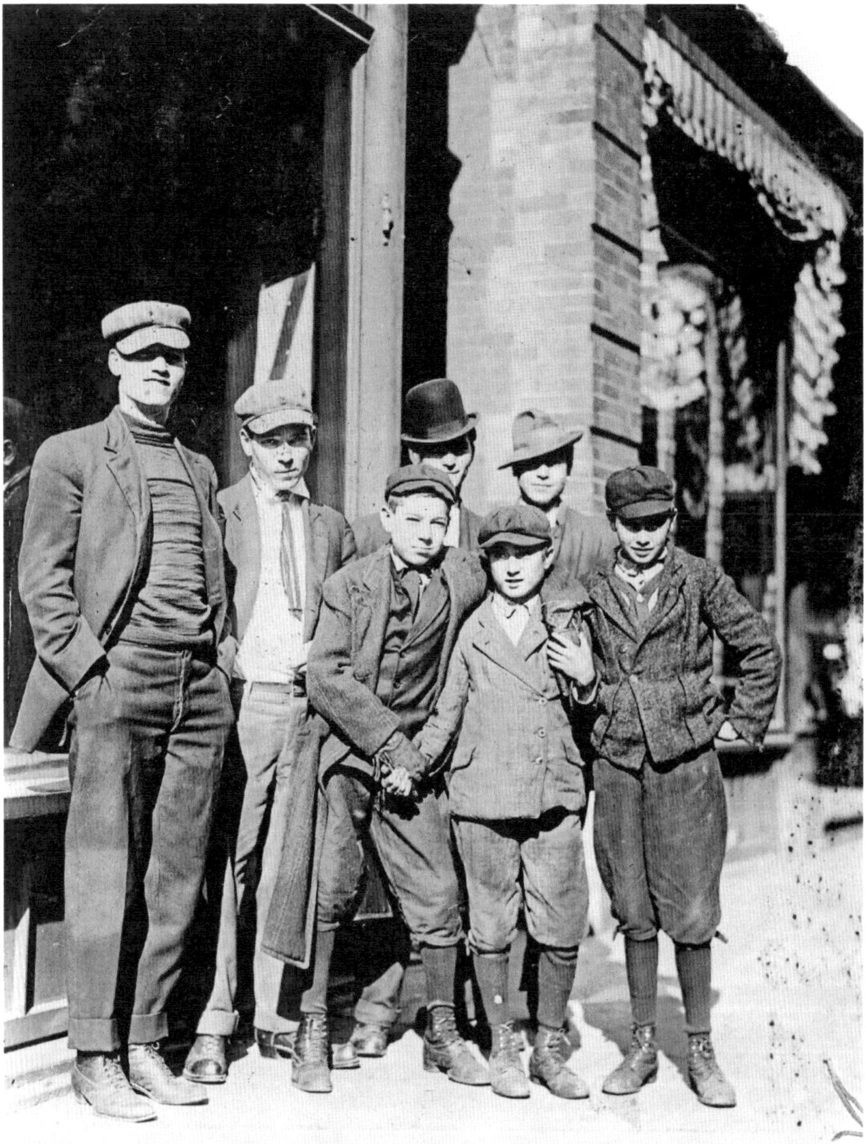

A group of unidentified Kibbe workers, photographed by Lewis Hine in 1910. *Library of Congress.*

candy per week, with 1,140 different varieties ranging from five-cent chocolate bars to the pricier gift boxes, which cost one to two dollars. Although primarily concentrated on the East Coast, Kibbe candies were sold across the country and even exported to Latin America, South Africa and Europe.

The future seemed promising for Kibbe, but as was the case with the Wason factory and many other Springfield businesses, it fell victim to the Great Depression. The bank foreclosed on the property in 1933, leaving several hundred people unemployed. The candy-making machinery was sold to other companies, and the buildings at the corner of Harrison Avenue and Dwight Street were demolished in 1935.

## LIBERTY BREWING COMPANY

Among the many future businessmen who came to Springfield during the nineteenth century was Theodor Geisel, a twenty-seven-year-old German immigrant who arrived in 1867. Although best known today as the grandfather of Dr. Seuss, he was a prominent citizen here in Springfield. In 1876, he and fellow German native Christian Kalmbach purchased a brewery on the outskirts of the city along State Street, where the MassMutual headquarters now stands, and formed Kalmbach & Geisel.

They were among the many nineteenth-century German immigrants who opened breweries in the United States, along with men like Adolphus Busch, Adolph Coors, Frederick Miller and Frederick Pabst. Even the brewery that Kalmbach & Geisel purchased had originally been built by Oscar Rocke, also from Germany.

Along with most other German brewers, Kalmbach & Geisel made lagers, which were popular in Germany but largely unknown in the United States until the mid-nineteenth century. Americans soon acquired a taste for this lighter style of beer, and from 1850 to 1890, per capita beer consumption in the United States increased from around one and a half gallons per year to over thirteen and a half gallons.

Here in Springfield, Kalmbach & Geisel capitalized on this sudden thirst for beer. When the partners purchased it, Rocke's old brewery could produce about one thousand barrels per year, but within ten years, their expanded facility had a capacity of over forty thousand barrels.

Theodor Geisel purchased Kalmbach's interest in the company in 1893 and renamed it Highland Brewing Company. Five years later, he sold it to the Springfield Brewing Company, but he did not leave the beer industry. In 1902, he and his son Theodor, Dr. Seuss's father, established the Liberty Brewing Company in a new building at the corner of Liberty and Charles Streets, just east of Chestnut Street.

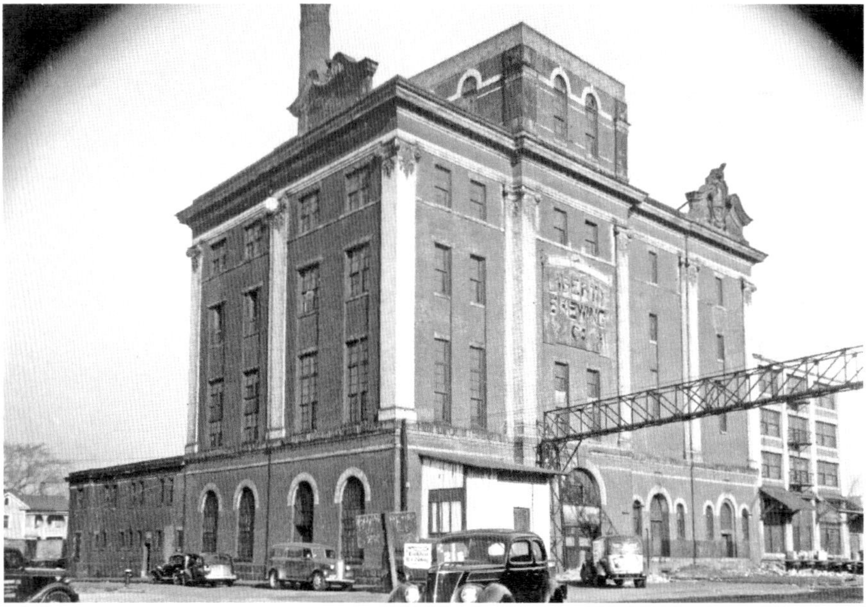

The Liberty Brewing Company building, around 1938–39. *Springfield Preservation Trust.*

In advertisements in the *Springfield Republican*, the Geisels emphasized the quality and purity of their beer, declaring in 1904, "The Superiority of the Liberty Brewing Co's Beer over the so-called 'Best beer' is acknowledged; and it is the natural result of a modern Brewery, No 1 Malt and Hops, the Excellence of Water and the Advanced Methods of the ART OF BREWING PROCESS."

The next year, the company posed the question "Do you know what you drink?" in its advertisements, which was followed by several paragraphs describing the purity of its beer, reassuring readers that Liberty beers did not contain adulterants such as "Salicylic or any other acid in any form." Instead, the Geisels used "Good Material, pure well water, brew[ed] it right and age[ed] it."

The Springfield Breweries Company purchased Liberty Brewing in 1913, and the elder Theodor Geisel retired. It was a good time for him to get out of the brewing business. The temperance movement had been growing in size and influence since the mid-nineteenth century, and by the early twentieth century, many were calling for national prohibition on all forms of alcohol. Aided in part by anti-German sentiment during World War I, the Eighteenth Amendment was ratified in 1919, banning "the manufacture, sale, or transportation of intoxicating liquors" in the United States.

Geisel died on December 5, 1919, at the age of seventy-nine, just six weeks before Prohibition went into effect. His son Theodor felt the effects of the new law, though. After the company merger in 1913, he became the general manager of Springfield Breweries and in 1920 became the president. Under his leadership, the company attempted to adapt to Prohibition; in an interview years later, Geisel told the *Springfield Union* that "nobody thought prohibition would last very long, and we tried to wait it out by selling soft drinks." The company made nonalcoholic beer in the old Liberty building, and it also introduced its own root beer. But these strategies failed, and Springfield Breweries soon closed for good.

Theodor Geisel found a new career, serving as the city's parks superintendent for thirty years, during which time his son, also named Theodor, became a prominent children's book author. As for the old family business, the former Liberty Brewing Company building remained vacant for the rest of Prohibition, and by the late 1930s, the property was purchased by Commonwealth Brewing Company. The company used the building as a distribution facility until 1945, when its owner, Leo Kaufman, was found guilty of adding fluorine as an adulterant to their beer.

Commonwealth closed after this, and the building remained vacant for the next two decades. In 1957, it was purchased by the Mansfield Paper Company, which later sold it to the Springfield Redevelopment Authority. Nearly fifty years after it produced its last beer, the old brewery was demolished in 1967 as part of the redevelopment of the North End, and the Springfield branch of the Registry of Motor Vehicles was built on part of the site.

# 5

# TAVERNS AND HOTELS

Because of Springfield's location at the crossroads of several important routes, it served as an important stop for travelers heading to and from Boston and other places in New England. It was situated on one of the three main routes of the Boston Post Road, which in colonial days connected Boston to New York and the rest of the colonies to the south. The first mail service along the route began in 1673, with the rider passing through Springfield during his two-week journey from New York to Boston.

Over a century later, Levi Pease started the first regular stagecoach line between Hartford and Boston, using the Boston Post Road for much of his route. Pease had been a blacksmith in Blandford, Massachusetts, before serving in the American Revolution. The war ended with the signing of the Treaty of Paris in September 1783, and a month later, Pease and his business partner Reuben Sikes began operating their stagecoach line.

The original route bypassed Springfield, and the partners found it difficult to get enough passengers until the following year, when they adjusted it to include a stop in Springfield. At first, passengers paid four pence per mile, which included up to fourteen pounds of baggage. The entire trip from Boston to Hartford cost ten dollars, but as the business improved, the fare was lowered to three pence per mile, and the stagecoach line was extended to New York, which was about six days from Boston.

Newspaper advertisements from the 1780s indicate that the Pease's stagecoaches did not schedule overnight stops in Springfield, but as the stagecoach industry grew in the late 1700s, so did the number of taverns in Springfield that accommodated travelers.

# PARSONS TAVERN

The most prominent of Springfield's early taverns was Parsons Tavern, which was originally situated on what is now the southeast corner of Court Square. The three-story building was owned by Zenas Parsons, whose grandfather Daniel Parsons had also been a licensed innkeeper in Springfield. Whether Daniel's tavern was in the same building is unclear, but by 1773, Zenas was operating his tavern here.

At the time, New England taverns served an important role in the town. Aside from providing lodging, food and drink, they were also a gathering place for locals to conduct business, discuss current events and hold meetings. For Springfield residents, there was much to discuss in Parsons Tavern in the early 1770s. Tensions were growing in Massachusetts over Britain's control of the colonies, but while Boston was the center of revolutionary talk, Springfield was far more subdued under the leadership of Colonel John Worthington, an influential Loyalist who served as one of the town selectmen. However, the Intolerable Acts increased anti-British sentiment in Springfield, and in August 1774, a large crowd gathered to protest in front of Parsons Tavern and forced Worthington and other Loyalists to swear that they would not seek public office again.

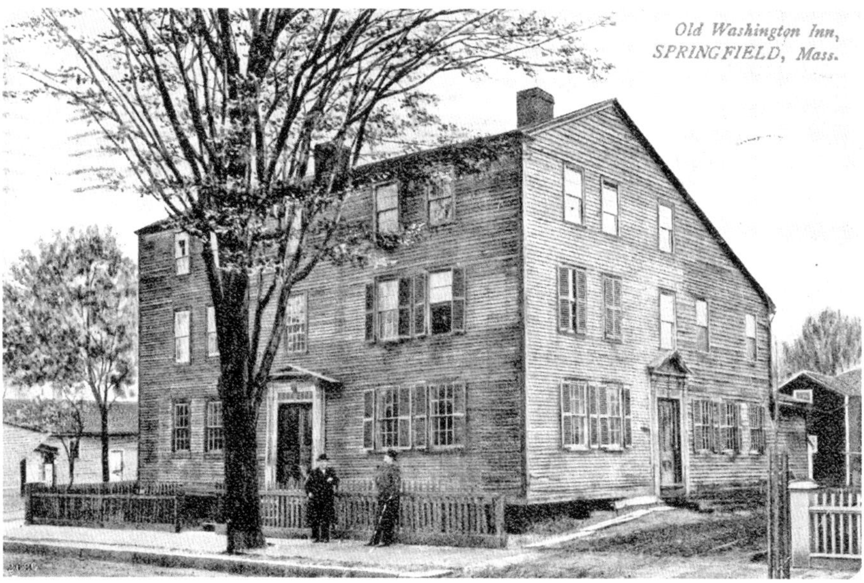


Early twentieth-century postcard showing Parsons Tavern at its location on Court Street in 1881. *Author's collection.*

As these protests were going on, the First Continental Congress was preparing to meet in Philadelphia to address the Intolerable Acts. Massachusetts sent John Adams, Samuel Adams, Thomas Cushing and Robert Treat Paine as delegates, and the group traveled together from Boston, staying overnight in Springfield on August 12. John Adams did not mention in his diary about whether they stayed at Parsons Tavern on their way to Philadelphia, but he did stop there for a meal on his way back home in November. In his November 5 entry, he wrote:

> *Dined at Parsons's of Springfield. Captn. Pynchon and another Pynchon, and Mr. Bliss, came in to see Us, and at last Coll. Worthington. Worthington behaved decently and politely. Said he was in Hopes we should have staid the Sabbath in Town and he should have had the Pleasure of waiting on us, &c. Captn. Pynchon was of the late provincial Congress and gave us some Account of their Proceedings.*

Less than a year later, another future president stopped at Parsons Tavern. While on his way to Cambridge to take command of the Continental army, George Washington, accompanied by General Charles Lee, made a brief stop at Parsons Tavern to meet Dr. Benjamin Church and Moses Gill before continuing toward Cambridge.

Fourteen years later, and less than six months after becoming president, Washington made a longer stop at Parsons Tavern, arriving on October 21, 1789, and inspecting the armory before staying overnight at the tavern. Just as Adams did many years earlier, Washington met with some of the town leaders, including John Worthington, who, despite his Loyalist sentiments, remained in Springfield after the war. In his diary, Washington wrote, "A Colo. Worthington, Colo. Williams (Adjutant General of the State of Massachusetts), Genl. Shepherd, Mr. Lyman and many other Gentlemen sat an hour or two with me in the evening at Parson's Tavern where I lodged and which is a good House."

John Adams also returned to Parsons Tavern during his presidency, stopping for dinner on his way from Brookfield to Suffield on November 14, 1798. By then, Zenas Parsons had retired and sold the building, but Adams appeared to enjoy his meal just as much, writing to his wife Abigail, "From Captain Draper at Brookfield we went to Springfield thirty one miles to dinner. Parsons has removed and a Mr Squire of Durham in Connecticutt [*sic*] has taken his house. We fared as well as usual and after Dinner crossed the River and reached this House Austins before sun sett."

By the start of the nineteenth century, the tavern was owned by Eleazer Williams, who was remembered years later for his interest in his personal appearance as well as for his slow, deliberate way of mixing drinks. His vanity apparently played a role in this leisurely demeanor; nearly a century later, Charles Wells Chapin described anecdotes about how Williams would stop in the middle of mixing a glass of toddy if he needed to fix his hair or brush off his clothing.

The role that the tavern played in the community during Williams's ownership extended far beyond just offering drinks and accommodations. Newspaper advertisements of the day indicate that it was the home of professional services such as a physician and a silhouette artist, and it was also a gathering place for events such as foreclosure sales and business meetings. The Proprietors of the Locks and Canals on the Connecticut River, who operated the South Hadley Canal, often met here, as did the Proprietors of the Springfield Bridge, who built the original bridge across the Connecticut River in Springfield.

By 1817, the tavern was owned by Captain John Bennett, and in June of that year, it had another presidential visit when James Monroe arrived during a tour of New England. A group of about sixty men escorted him from the state line to the tavern, where he was greeted with a speech by Timothy Dwight before traveling up the hill to inspect the armory. Following the inspection, he returned to the tavern, where a crowd of over four hundred local schoolchildren waited to see him. He ate dinner at the tavern and then continued on his trip back to Connecticut, where he was again escorted back to the state line.

A few years after Monroe's visit, the tavern was sold again, to Erastus Chapin. By this time, though, the building's future was in question. The new First Church building had just been completed nearby, and there were plans underway to build a new county courthouse next to it, with a public square in front. This would have involved removing the tavern, which Chapin initially objected to.

Chapin eventually sold the property in exchange for $3,000 plus property just to the north, at the corner of Main and West Court Streets. In swapping the old colonial tavern, he was able to build a modern brick hotel on his new property, which had a desirable location at the heart of downtown and across from the new Court Square. In announcing its opening, Chapin advertised that "it is deemed by competent judges to be the most commodious building of the kind in the state, west of Boston" and, perhaps most importantly, "The Choicest Liquors will at all times be kept; and during the summer months a SODA FOUNTAIN will be attached to the establishment." However, Chapin seemed to have had little success with the hotel; he soon sold it and moved west, first to Albany, where he ran a hotel for a few years, and then to St. Louis, where he apparently gave up on the hotel business and became a flour and grain dealer.

The old tavern, meanwhile, was split into two parts and moved off the land that would become Court Square. The smaller section was used as a boardinghouse and moved around several times. By 1858, it was on the western part of Union Street, and as the *Springfield Republican* described it at the time, it was "a comfortable receptacle for Irish families."

The larger, more prominent section of the tavern was moved a short distance away to the north side of West Court Street, just to the west of where Symphony Hall now stands. There, the building that had once housed three of the first five presidents was divided into a four-family tenement house. Its historical significance did not go unnoticed by the people of Springfield, though. Part of the city's 250th anniversary celebrations in 1886 included a dance in the tavern's old hall, and a decade later, the owners offered to sell the building to anyone willing to preserve it. In 1897, the *Springfield Republican* estimated that it was about 150 years old and probably the second-oldest building in the city, but there was not enough interest to raise sufficient funds, so it was demolished in September 1897 and replaced by a brick apartment building.

## WARRINER'S TAVERN

Another early tavern was located at the southwest corner of Main and State Streets. The house itself was built around 1773, and from 1815 to 1820, it was operated as a tavern by Elijah Goodrich. It was in a good location, situated in the center of the town and right on the stagecoach road to Boston, but Goodrich was apparently more interested in horses than tavern keeping. He moved to a more spacious location farther up State Street, where he trained fast horses, and he sold the tavern to Thomas Bates.

Bates's daughter Phoebe and her husband, Jeremy Warriner, later took over its operation, adding a third floor and making it one of Springfield's finest hotels of the early nineteenth century. It was an important stagecoach stop, but it was equally popular with locals, who affectionately referred to the couple as Uncle Jerry and Aunt Phoebe.

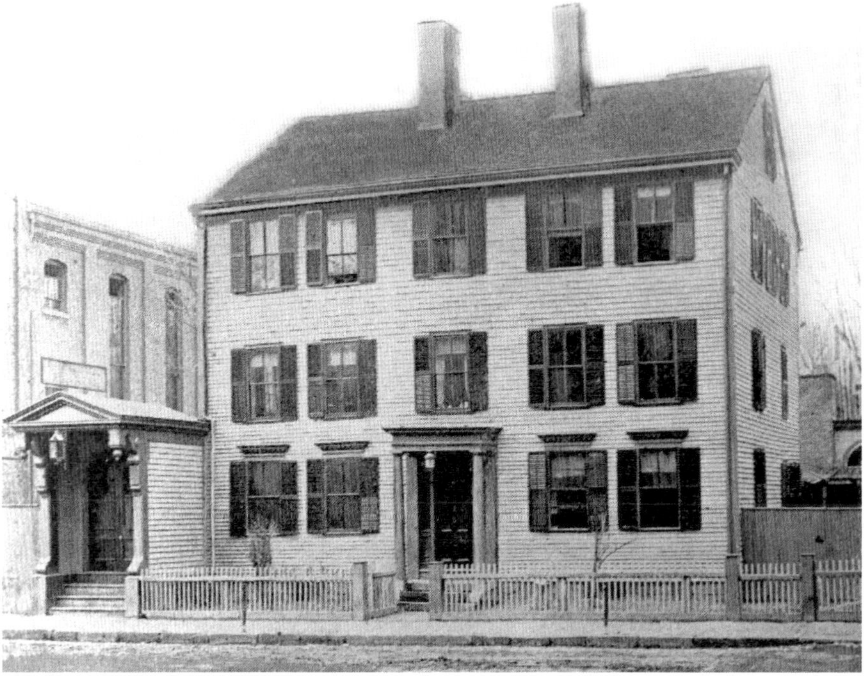

Warriner's Tavern in the late nineteenth century, after its relocation to State Street. *From* Sketches of the Old Inhabitants and Other Citizens of Old Springfield, *1893.*

Part of the tavern's popularity was due to Phoebe's cooking, which was described a half century later in *King's Handbook of Springfield* as "a matter of jealousy to housewives and a marvel to husbands." Popular writer and poet Sara Jane Lippincott, who used the pen name Grace Greenwood, wrote a glowing review of Phoebe's meals after a visit in 1849, "I am not about to attempt a description of Warriner's dinner, with their endless succession of delicious dishes, their inimitable sauces, and exquisite puddings and pastry. For this I have neither time nor talent sufficient." Of all the dishes, though, she was most impressed with the broiled chicken: "Why, I had never before conceived to what a state of rare deliciousness that juvenile domestic fowl might be exalted by skillful cookery. I had never eaten broiled chicken before, and whoever, not having breakfasted at Warriner's, believes himself acquainted with broiled chicken, labors under a melancholy mistake."

However, Warriner's tavern was certainly not patronized exclusively for the food. By the 1830s, the temperance movement was growing in popularity in Springfield and around the country, and some 2,500 of the town's 6,784 residents had joined the Springfield Temperance Society by 1834. Despite this, though, about 11,500 gallons of rum alone had been sold in Springfield the previous year, much of which was probably consumed at Warriner's. *King's Handbook* described the tavern's bar as "the rendezvous of all the wild and reckless youngsters of the day," but it was also frequented by the more respectable members of Springfield society, who, as Alfred Minot Copeland described in his 1902 *History of Hampden County*, "had a keen appreciation of Uncle Jerry's toddies and slings. No severe winter cold could withstand the potent effects of one of these decoctions."

As lucrative as the tavern was for Jeremy Warriner, it also served as a convenient front for his involvement in the Underground Railroad. He would sometimes have eight to ten runaway slaves hiding in the hotel at any given time, and he also employed many of them. Mary Sly, who ran away from Natchez, Mississippi, worked here for many years, as did her daughter Julia, who was born at the tavern. Many years later, in an interview with the *Springfield Homestead*, Julia recalled her time working here:

> *Jane Hall and I helped wait on table. I used to feel quite proud when some of those big folks would come in on the stage and when they'd sit down at the table would say, "Where's Julia, I want Julia to wait on me." Those folks were generous about tipping, too. They would leave money around under the plates, often 25 cents and sometimes as much as a dollar.*

A dollar tip was no small sum in the 1840s, with Julia waiting on some of the most prominent public figures of the era. She went on to explain:

> *I used to know some of the biggest folks in the country. Daniel Webster would stop over on his way to and from Boston. Webster always had a parlor and bedroom. I used to carry his meals up to his room. He kept by himself a good deal and was always busy. Rufus Choate used to come here, too. My! How that man would walk the floor. Lots of brides used to come and we had bridal chambers for them. They would send on ahead for rooms and sometimes Jerry would have the band come and serenade them at night. I couldn't begin to tell all the people who would come. Mrs. Harriet Beecher Stowe I remember and Mrs. Samuel Colt of Hartford, and Fanny Elsley, the great dancer, and Henry Clay, I most forgot him, and P.T. Barnum and Jennie Lind and Louis Kossuth.*

One particularly notable visit for Julia was that of Elizabeth Bonaparte, the ex-wife of Napoleon's youngest brother:

> *It was this way: Mrs. Jerome Bonaparte of Baltimore had a head waiter, William Gordon, who ran away and came up north….Well, this Gordon, was in our house, when who should appear but Mrs. Bonaparte and her family. They knew their waiter was up north somewhere and my! the fuss they made, but they didn't get their slave. Uncle Jerry was too smart for them.*

Throughout the 1830s, Warriner's Tavern was Springfield's leading hotel, but its supremacy began to wane with the completion of the railroad a half mile to the north in 1839. The days of the stagecoach were numbered, and Warriner soon faced stiff competition from the Massasoit House, located directly adjacent to the railroad depot.

Around 1846, Warriner, who was sixty-two at this point, sold the old colonial-era building and moved his business a block south to the corner of Main and Bliss Streets, where he opened the Union House. It was located in a new brick building, and he had no problem attracting distinguished guests. In 1847, President James K. Polk spent the night there with a group that

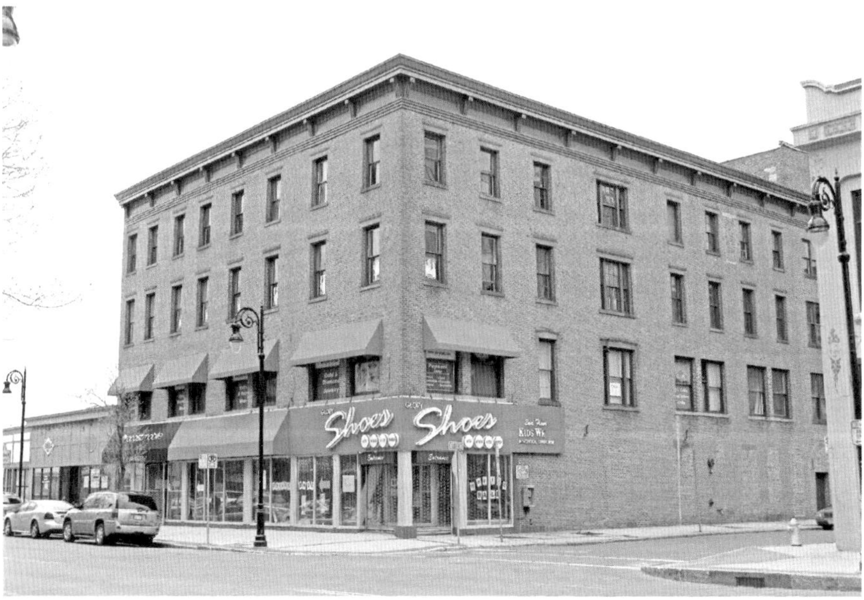


The old Union House building in 2015, shortly before it closed. *Author's collection.*

included future president James Buchanan, who was secretary of state at the time. It was also here, two years later, that Sara Jane Lippincott visited and feasted on the broiled chicken. However, the hotel still had the same problem of being too far from the railroad, and the Warriners were never particularly satisfied in their new location, so they retired a few years later.

The old building at the corner of Main and State Streets was moved a little to the west along State Street in 1847, where it continued to be used as a hotel. It stood there for the next sixty years, before it was demolished in in 1907 to build the United Electric Company Building.

After the Warriners retired, the Union House building changed hands—and names—several times before becoming the Chandler Hotel in the late 1880s. The hotel closed in the 1930s, and the building saw a variety of other uses over the years. Much of it was demolished in 2016 as part of the MGM Springfield casino project, but the Main Street façade is being preserved and will be incorporated into the casino design.

## MASSASOIT HOUSE

Springfield's most famous nineteenth-century hotel was the Massasoit House, located on Main Street just south of the railroad arch. It was started in 1843 by Marvin Chapin, who at first glance would have seemed like an unlikely candidate to start a nationally renowned hotel.

Born in 1806 in Somers, Connecticut, Chapin was the son of a farmer, and early in life he worked on the family farm before apprenticing as a tanner and shoemaker. However, he had difficulty staying on one career path. After his three-year apprenticeship, Chapin briefly worked as a tanner, then as a store clerk, and he even joined a surveying crew that traveled to Florida to survey a railroad route.

After returning from Florida, Chapin entered the hotel business, working first as a clerk at the Cabot House in Chicopee before purchasing it. He briefly tried to start a papermaking business in Westfield, but this venture failed and he soon returned to the Cabot House. It was not long, though, before Chapin seized on another business opportunity. When the Western Railroad opened its depot in 1839, Chapin was one of the first to recognize the effect that it would have on Springfield's businesses.

John Hooker had been one of Springfield's leading citizens in the early nineteenth century, serving as town selectman and, for the last sixteen years of his life, as judge of probate. He died in 1829, and after his widow's death in 1842, their house on the west side of Main Street, just south of the new railroad depot, was put up for auction. Chapin saw the potential that the location offered for a hotel and formed a partnership with Israel Parsons. Together, they purchased the property for $8,000.

They moved John Hooker's old house to the western side of the lot, where it later became a hotel as well, and they began construction at the corner of Main Street and present-day Gridiron Street. Parsons soon backed out of it, though, and sold his share of the business to Chapin, who in turn recruited his younger brother Ethan to take his place. The two brothers formed the partnership of M. & E.S. Chapin, and they opened their hotel on June 26, 1843, as the Massasoit House, named for the Wampanoag chief who had assisted the Pilgrims in Plymouth.

From the start, the Massasoit House was a success. In addition to providing overnight lodging for visitors to Springfield, the hotel's proximity to the railroad also made it an ideal place for hungry passengers to stop for a quick meal before continuing on their journey. The meals were particularly popular thanks to the Marvin and Ethan's sister, Roxanna Chapin, who worked as the hotel's chef in the early years. Her specialties included desserts, such as custards, pies and puddings, that were said to have rivaled even those of Phoebe Warriner.

Although the hotel started small, it soon expanded. In 1847, the Chapins completed a wood-frame addition to the south along Main Street, and six years later, they added a brick section to the rear of the original building. The 1847 addition was torn down in 1857 and replaced with a more permanent brick building, giving the hotel a total of 130 guest rooms and a dining room that could seat 150, along with other public rooms such as parlors, a smoking room and a reading room.

The Chapins soon discovered that, for many travelers, money was no object. While locals could eat for thirty-seven and a half cents per meal, out-of-town guests were charged fifty cents for the same meal. This was a significant amount of money, but they eventually raised their prices to one dollar, finding that people were still willing to pay. One nineteenth-century account relates that a guest who had stayed in the hotel's finest room for a week was given a bill for thirty-five dollars at checkout. The Chapins were hesitant about giving someone a bill for such a princely sum, but the man paid it without blinking.

In its heyday, the guests at the Massasoit House included some of the most prominent people of the mid-nineteenth century. Presidents Franklin

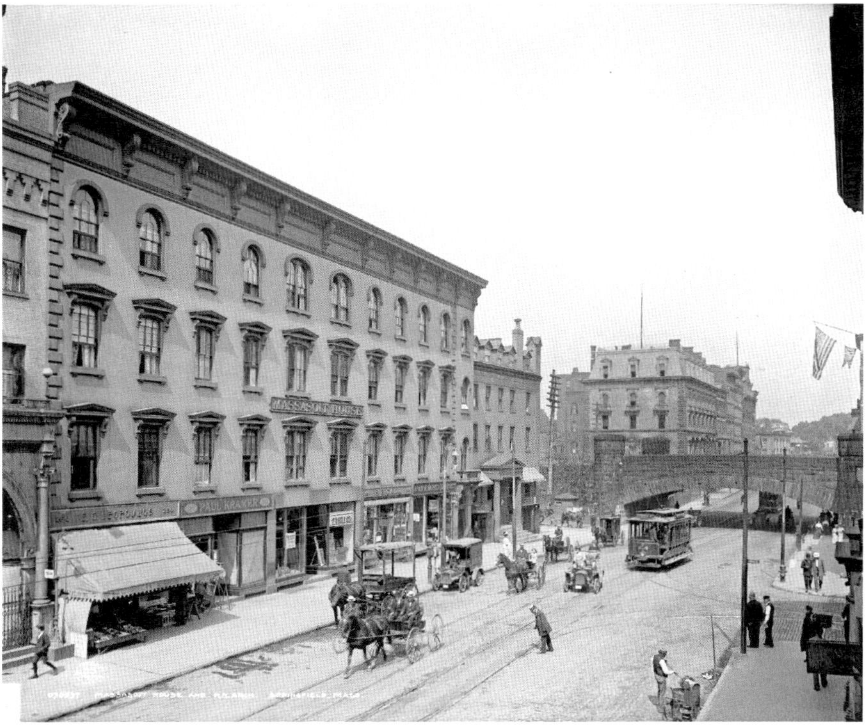


The Massasoit House around 1908, with the 1850s addition on the left and the original building beyond it in the center. *Library of Congress.*

Pierce, Andrew Johnson and Ulysses S. Grant all stopped here, as did twenty-two-year-old Theodore Roosevelt and his first wife, Alice, who spent their wedding night here after their marriage in Brookline. The hotel also saw other notable politicians, such as Henry Clay, Daniel Webster, William Seward and Stephen Douglas, plus Civil War generals William T. Sherman and George B. McClellan. Abolitionist John Brown, who lived in Springfield for a time, was known to visit, and even future Confederate president Jefferson Davis stayed here during an inspection of the Springfield Armory while he was secretary of war. Other guests have included poets and authors such as Henry Wadsworth Longfellow, Ralph Waldo Emerson, Oliver Wendell Holmes and Charles Dickens.

The hotel was also the site of a series of historic meetings held between 1876 and 1882. Although widely known as the birthplace of basketball, Springfield also played an important role in the development of football. Prior to 1876, there were no standardized rules for college football, and each school played under different rules, with some resembling modern soccer while others were based on rugby rules. In an effort to reach an agreement, representatives from Harvard, Yale, Princeton and Columbia met at the Massasoit House on November 23, 1876.

At the convention, the delegates agreed to adopt rugby-style football as opposed to soccer, and they wrote sixty-one new rules that formed the basis for modern American football. One area of contention, though, which would be surprising to modern football fans, was whether or not touchdowns would count toward the score. At this time, the focus was on kicking goals, and the kick that followed touchdowns—today's extra point kick—was valued more than the touchdown itself. Ultimately, one of the sixty-one rules that they adopted was a compromise, which scored a touchdown as one fourth of a field goal.

In the years that followed, college football figures continued to meet regularly at the Massasoit House, with Yale's halfback Walter Camp becoming a dominant fixture there. Known as the "Father of American Football," Camp helped move the game further away from its rugby roots, and under his influence at the meetings, new rules were added, such as establishing the line of scrimmage and having eleven players on each side. These rules meetings at the Massasoit House continued through 1882, and during this time, Springfield played an integral role in the formation of modern American football.

Under the Chapins' management, the Massasoit House generally ran smoothly. With Roxanna in charge of the food, the brothers split up the other responsibilities: Marvin handled the finances, while Ethan oversaw the maintenance and improvements to the building. Their business model focused more on substance over form, choosing, for example, to serve a limited menu of simple, high-quality food rather than offering a wide variety of substandard options. As the *Springfield Republican*

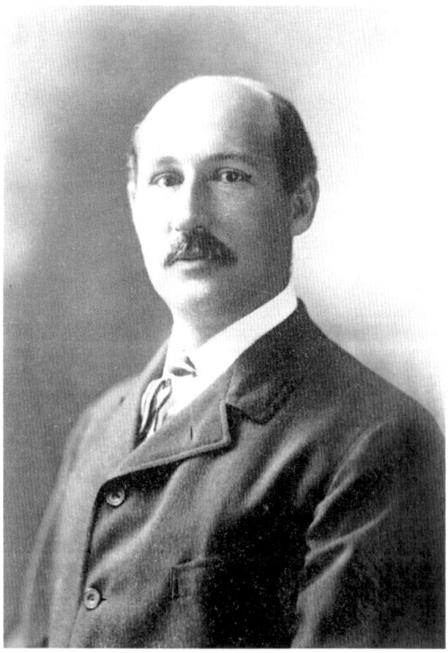

Walter Camp, a fixture at many of the Massasoit Conventions, photographed in the early twentieth century. *Library of Congress.*

described it in 1912, "The fame of the Massasoit house was never based upon sumptuous elegance. It was rather a place where one went and found himself excellently fed, so comfortably housed and in surroundings of such congeniality that the charm was irresistible."

Thanks to the success of the Massasoit House, the Chapins were among Springfield's leading citizens in the second half of the nineteenth century. In 1851, Marvin and Ethan were two of the original investors in the Springfield Fire and Marine Insurance Company, contributing $15,000 to the company. In addition to serving as a director of the insurance company, Marvin was also a director and later president of the Springfield Gas Light Company, and he was president of the Agawam National Bank from 1862 to 1870.

Marvin and Ethan retired in 1886, turning the management of the hotel over to their nephew, William H. Chapin, who first leased the property before purchasing it outright in 1892. Ethan died in 1889 at the age of seventy-five, and Marvin died ten years later at the age of ninety-two.

William Chapin owned the property until 1912, when he sold it for $750,000 in what was at the time the largest real estate transaction in the city's history. The new owners continued to operate the hotel, but they made some substantial changes along the way. The façade along Main Street and Gridiron Street was rebuilt in the popular Classical Revival style of the era, and the hotel rooms in the section facing Main Street were replaced with offices, leaving only the hotel rooms on the north side of the building along Gridiron Street.

More changes came in 1926, when the hotel closed after eighty-three years of operation. The remaining hotel rooms were converted into offices, and the building was expanded in the back to add the Paramount Theater. When completed in 1929, it was considered the finest movie theater in western Massachusetts, but it was also used for vaudeville performances, plays and concerts. Just as the Massasoit House had attracted distinguished guests in the previous century, the Paramount Theater saw live performances from some of the premier entertainers of the day, including Ethel Barrymore, Frank Sinatra and Nat King Cole.

However, by the 1960s, the theater was seeing only occasional use. In 1975, the owners attempted to rebrand it by renaming it in honor of Broadway star and Springfield native Julia Sanderson. Another revival effort came in 1999, when it was reopened as the Hippodrome nightclub. As of 2016, it is no longer used as a nightclub, and it has been renamed the Paramount Theater. Much of the historic interior of the theater remains intact, but as has been the case for the past fifty years, it remains in use only sporadically.

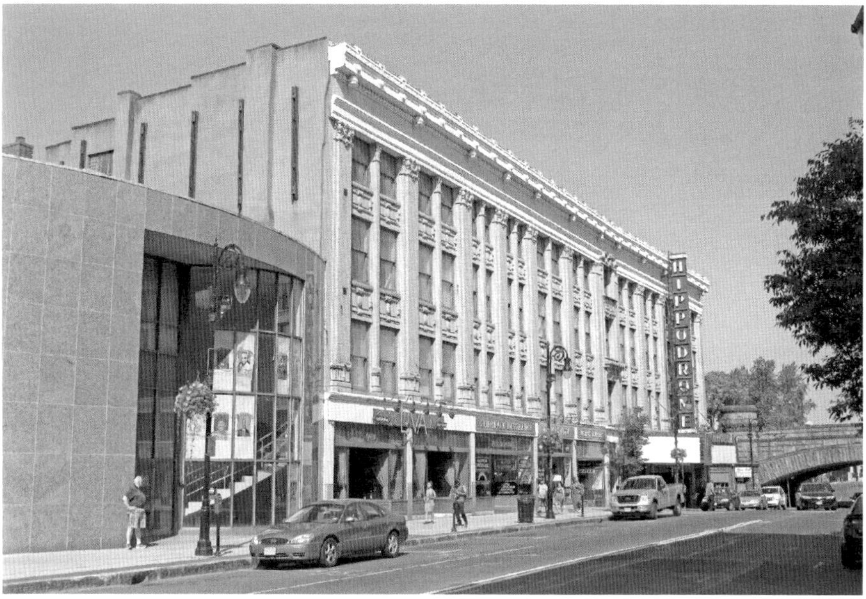


The Paramount Theater from Main Street in 2016. *Author's collection.*

Despite the drastic alterations over the years, though, there are still parts of the old Massasoit House that have survived, hidden behind the 1912 façade. In particular, the southern part of the building along Main Street still has some of the original features, including the marble fireplaces that date back to its days as a grand hotel. However, aside from the first-floor storefronts, most of the historic building has been vacant for many years and is in need of restoration.

## VICTORIA HOTEL

This building that once stood at the northwest corner of State and Dwight Streets was originally the first YMCA building in the city. The five-story Romanesque structure was completed in 1895, and aside from dormitory rooms for young men, it included recreational facilities such as a pool, two bowling alleys and a gymnasium with weights, climbing ropes, punching bags, a running track and "basket ball outfits." With such a building, the organization was able to provide a safe environment for young men, away from drinking, gambling, theaters and women. As explained in the *Springfield Republican* when the building first opened, "[I]t is possible to compete with the saloon and furnish a place where the members sometimes shall be able to sleep, eat and derive all their social pleasures and edification from such a home."

It did not take the YMCA long to outgrow the building, and in 1915, it moved to a new location on Chestnut Street. The twenty-year-old building was sold and became the Victoria Hotel, which served both transient guests as well as permanent residents. The 1920 census shows thirty-seven living here at the time, twenty men and seventeen women. There were four married couples and one mother and daughter living together, but otherwise the other residents lived alone. Aside from the sixteen-year-old who lived with her mother, everyone was over twenty-three and most were in their forties or older. Most were employed, with occupations that included maids, salesmen, clerks and even a lawyer and an aviator.

It was never the one of the city's finest hotels, but things only got worse after 1921, when it sustained heavy damage in a streetcar accident. In the

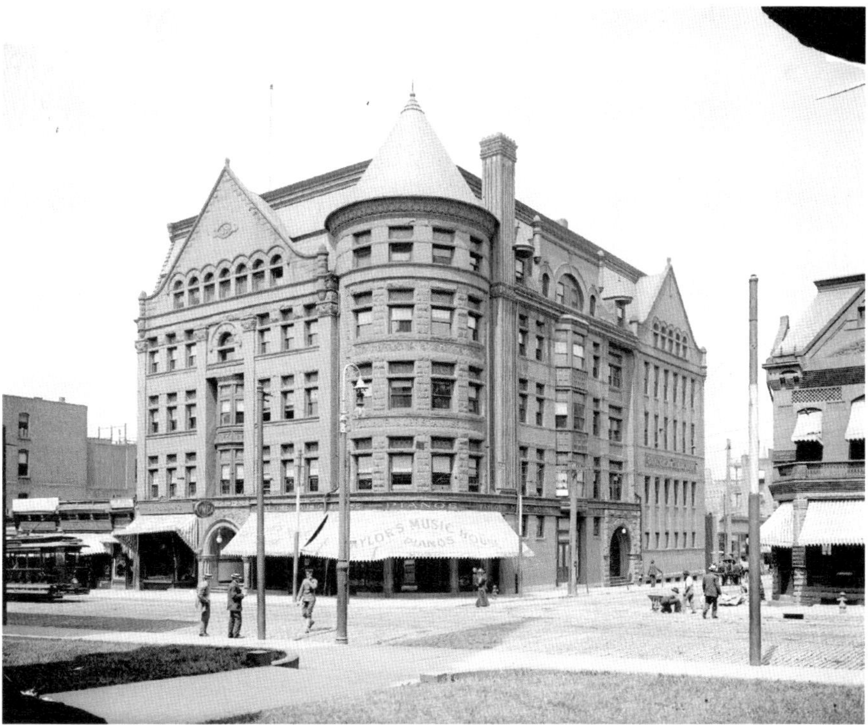

The YMCA Building, which later became the Victoria Hotel, around 1900–10. *Library of Congress.*

early morning hours of August 31, three freight trolley cars were traveling down the tracks on State Street when they derailed at the intersection of Dwight Street. The cars, which were carrying an assortment of meat, fish, dry goods and other freight, crashed into the corner of the hotel, demolishing the storefront of the Superior Candy Company and causing the rounded corner wall to collapse.

There were about one hundred guests asleep in the hotel at the time, including John A. Simpson, a salesman from Gloversville, New York, who described his experience to the *Republican*:

> *I was asleep at the time. I was awakened by what seemed like a blinding flash and roar at the same time—it appeared as though the whole city was being blown up. My first thought was that the end of the world had come. Everything in my room, of course, was pitch dark. I was probably struck on the head when the ceiling fell in—then the next thing I knew someone called out, "Is it all right in there?"*

He was found on the floor beside his bed, covered in blood and ceiling plaster, and brought to the hospital, where he was treated for a head wound and some abrasions. There were no deaths from the accident, but several others were hospitalized for their injuries, including Abraham Boiriso, who was on the trolley at the time. He was pinned under the wreckage for over an hour but suffered only minor bruises.

Ultimately, the accident could have been much worse, but further disaster was prevented by two steel columns that supported the corner of the building. They had been added during renovations after the YMCA sold it, and they likely prevented the entire structure from collapsing. The candy shop was heavily damaged, as were several other businesses in the basement and first floor, but the hotel itself escaped serious damage. Six rooms were destroyed, but hotel operator Eleanor Garrick told the *Republican* that the rest were in usable condition.

The damage to the building was repaired within a few months, but its decline continued. It remained primarily a hotel for long-term tenants, with a 1937 classified advertisement describing it as "very comfortable and pleasant, full hotel service" with one floor reserved for women. The weekly rent of three dollars for permanent guests included a room with running water and a telephone. Some rooms had private bathrooms, and for the rest there were communal bathrooms on each floor.

The building was renovated in 1964 with secondhand furnishings from the nearby Sheraton-Kimball Hotel, but just a few years later, the ninety-six-

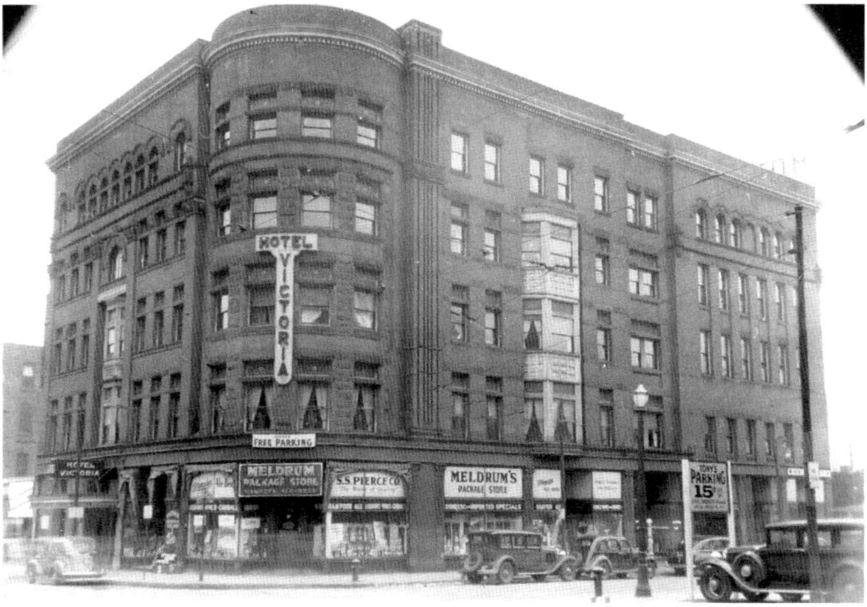


The somewhat reconstructed YMCA Building during its time as the Victoria Hotel, around 1938–39. *Springfield Preservation Trust.*

room hotel housed just forty permanent guests. It was targeted for demolition to build the Civic Center, but in the meantime, arsonists did their best to destroy it. In the spring of 1968, eight small fires were started in the building, including one that caused considerable damage to the fifth floor. One of the residents was charged for the fires, but the following year, another man started a second-floor fire that permanently closed the hotel. It remained vacant until its demolition in December 1969, and the site of the hotel is now the southeast corner of the MassMutual Center.

6

# HOUSES

In his inaugural address to the city council in January 1887, Mayor Elisha B. Maynard concluded with a remark about Springfield's newly acquired nickname of the "City of Homes." At the time, the city was in the middle of a population boom, and Maynard explained that many were drawn here by Springfield's "central location, its schools, its social advantages and its general attractiveness." There were also plenty of jobs here, especially for skilled laborers and other middle-class workers, so while other New England cities were building large tracts of factory tenements, Springfield was building hundreds of upscale single-family homes.

Springfield is still referred to as the City of Homes, and many of its historic houses are still standing, including the mansions on Maple Street, the late nineteenth- and early twentieth-century homes of the Forest Park neighborhood and the eight hundred Queen Anne–style homes of the McKnight Historic District. However, over the years Springfield has also lost a number of significant houses. Some were renowned for their architectural value, and others were home to historical figures of national significance, but they have since been lost through fire, neglect, urban renewal or apathy.

## Ely Ordinary

When Maynard gave his speech in 1887, one of the city's oldest homes was located a few blocks away from city hall, at the corner of Dwight and Sanford

Streets. Probably the last surviving seventeenth-century building in the city, it dated back to at least 1665 and was originally owned by Nathaniel Ely, an early settler who emigrated from England in 1634 and came to Springfield in 1659.

The house was originally located on Main Street at the southwest corner of Bliss Street, and in 1665, Ely was granted a license to operate an "ordinary," or tavern, in the building. The license gave him permission to "keepe ordinary there, or house for common Entertaynment…as also for selling wines and strong liquors, for ye year ensuing, Provided he keep good rule and order in the house." He ran the tavern until his death in 1675, but he did find himself in court several times. In 1667, he was fined sixteen pounds for "selling four quarts of cider to the Indians," and seven years later he was fined forty shillings for selling watered-down beer. The laws at the time required beer to have a "rate of 4 bushels of good barley malt" per hogshead, but the court found "this beere farr below that rule in ye law."

After Ely's death, the building was used as a private residence for well over 150 years, and by the 1820s, it was the home of Dr. Joseph Stone, a physician who practiced medicine in Greenfield, New York City and Providence before coming to Springfield around 1821. After his death in 1838, the property was sold. At this point, its location on Main Street was valuable commercial real estate, so the house was moved and Warriner's Union House built on the site.

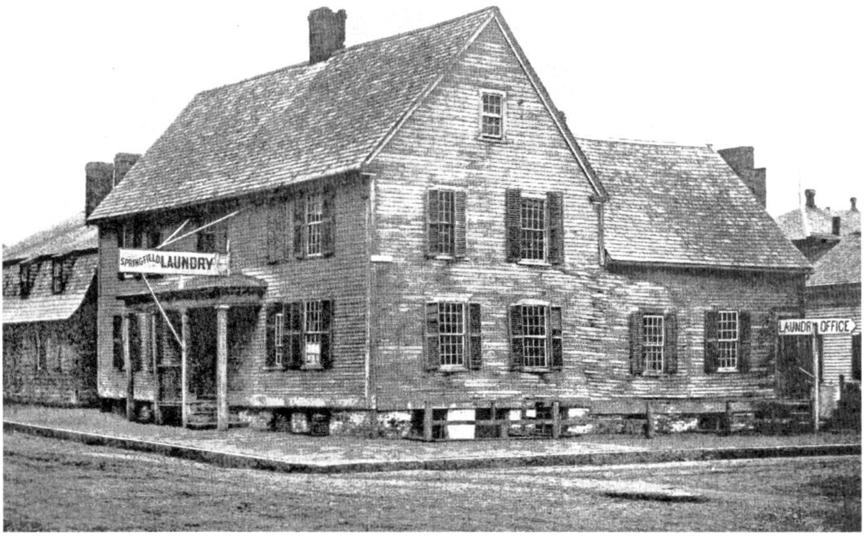


The Ely Ordinary at the corner of Dwight and Sanford Streets, in 1878. *From* A History of Hampden County, Massachusetts, *1902*.

The old Ely Ordinary was moved to Dwight Street, joining the nearby 1723 courthouse as another once-prominent colonial building that had been relegated to the back streets. Here, it fell into gradual decline and disrepair. By 1874, the first floor was the Springfield Laundry, with tenements on the second floor. It eventually became uninhabitable, though, with leaking roofs, collapsing chimneys and dangerous stairs. In 1899, the owners of the mostly vacant building were planning to redevelop the property, and they offered the historic building to anyone who was willing to move it to a new location. Despite decades of neglect, it still retained much of its colonial-era appearance. The *Springfield Republican* described it this way:

> *An extremely narrow "stoop" is attached to the front from which one enters the low, dingy inner hall through thick-cased doors. The ceilings are less than eight feet high, the windows, though small, have 32 panes of glass each. From the narrow hall, a steep flight of stairs leads to an equally narrow upper hall. The lower rooms are fitted with fireplaces, or the remains of them, for several generations of small boys have pestered neighbors' cats with bricks from their walls. The floors are of wide boards and coarse lumber and they, too, are probably of later date than the building itself. The bar-room in which Ely sold ye ancient beere is still intact.*

Over 240 years old at this point, the building was recognized as probably the oldest in the city, and its relatively small size would have made moving it far easier than Parsons Tavern, which had been in a similar situation only a couple years earlier. However, the Ely Ordinary was in such poor condition that it was impractical to save, and it was demolished in June 1900. The brick building that replaced it was subsequently demolished in 1960, and the site of the old house is now part of the MassMutual Center.

## DWIGHT HOUSE

Another colonial home that survived for many years was the Dwight House, built around 1764 for Josiah Dwight, a member of Springfield's prominent Dwight family. He had a number of roles in the community, including town selectman, judge on the county's Court of Common Pleas and lieutenant colonel in the militia. His house was located on the west side of Main Street, between Bliss and Howard Streets, and it reflected both his standing within the community and also his substantial wealth, which included five thousand acres of land.

At his death in 1768, Josiah Dwight's estate was valued at over £9,000, and his eldest son, Thomas, inherited his father's mansion. Thomas graduated from Harvard in 1778 and practiced law in Springfield, where he married Hannah Worthington in 1791. Like Thomas, she came from a prominent family; her father was Colonel John Worthington, and her mother was the niece of Jonathan Edwards.

In addition to his law practice, he had a significant political career. He was a perennial member of the board of selectmen, and during this time, he was also elected to the state House of Representatives from 1794 to 1795, the state Senate from 1796 to 1803 and 1813, the U.S. House of Representatives from 1803 to 1805 and the Governor's Council from 1808 to 1809. One of the more interesting moments from his time in Congress came in 1803, when the House voted to authorize funds for the Louisiana Purchase. At less than three cents per acre, it was a bargain price, but Dwight was one of twenty-five who voted against it, fearing that westward expansion would reduce New England's influence over the country.

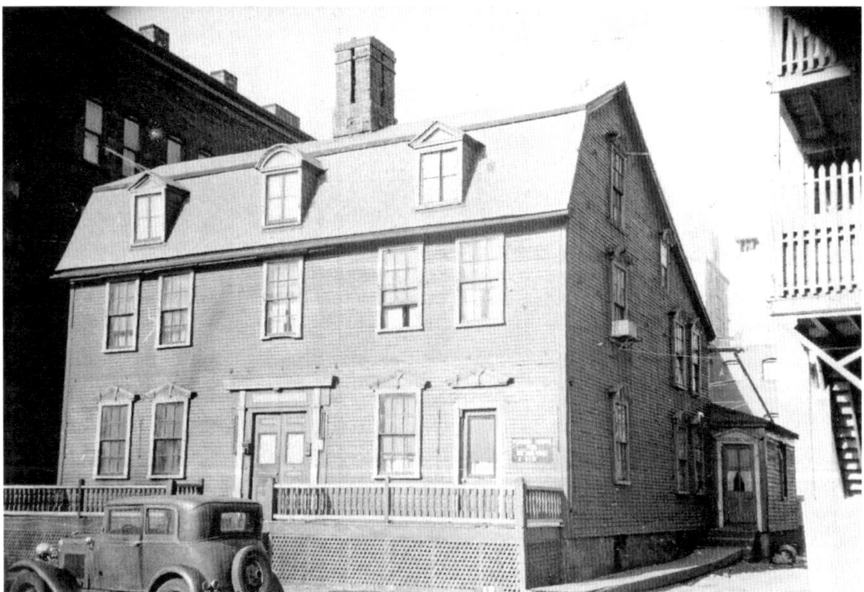

The Dwight House around 1938–39, during its time as a tenement house. *Springfield Preservation Trust.*

Dwight died in 1819, and later in the century, his house was moved around the corner to the north side of Howard Street. The large building became a two-unit tenement house, but it still retained much of its original colonial appearance. By the turn of the century, it was completely surrounded by modern brick buildings and owned by George J. Seuss, the maternal grandfather of Dr. Seuss. He lived a few houses away and rented out the old Dwight House. It remained in his family for years after his death in 1901, and census records from the early twentieth century show that it was primarily rented to immigrants, including families from Ireland, Quebec and Italy.

In 1917, the *Springfield Republican* identified it as the last remaining colonial-era building in the city. It had gone from a congressman's mansion to a tenement house, but the newspaper noted "the real beauty and dignity of its simplicity, the charm which is about it in spite of its being somewhat dilapidated," and that, surrounded by modern buildings, it "stands there in its alien atmosphere with a forlorn sort of look as if thinking of its better days."

A little over thirty years later, the house had deteriorated to the point where it needed to be torn down. However, it was purchased by Henry Flint of Historic Deerfield, who had the house meticulously dismantled board by board. Even the old nails were saved, and several years later, it was rebuilt about thirty miles away in Deerfield, where it still stands alongside a number of other restored historic houses.

## JOHN BROWN HOUSE

Perhaps no Springfield resident of the nineteenth century had a greater impact on American history than abolitionist John Brown. Born in Torrington, Connecticut, in 1800, Brown spent most of his early life in Ohio, where he became a strong opponent of slavery. He was particularly influenced by the 1837 murder of abolitionist Elijah Lovejoy. In a church prayer meeting held in the aftermath of Lovejoy's death, John Brown stood and declared, "Here, before God, in the presence of these witnesses, from this time, I consecrate my life to the destruction of slavery!"

In the years that followed, Brown embarked on several different business ventures, and in 1846, he came to Springfield as a wool merchant. With business partner Simon Perkins, he established Perkins & Brown, with offices and a warehouse near the Massasoit House and the railroad depot.

In 1847, Brown and his family moved into a house on Hastings Street, which later became Franklin Street, in the newly developing North End. Its Greek Revival design was typical of many other houses that were being built in Springfield around this time, with little to distinguish it architecturally from the surrounding homes in this working-class neighborhood. This was noted by abolitionist Frederick Douglass, who visited the home in November 1847. Reflecting on his visit, Douglass wrote that he first saw Brown's offices, which gave "the impression that the owner must be a man of considerable wealth." His home, though, was quite a contrast:

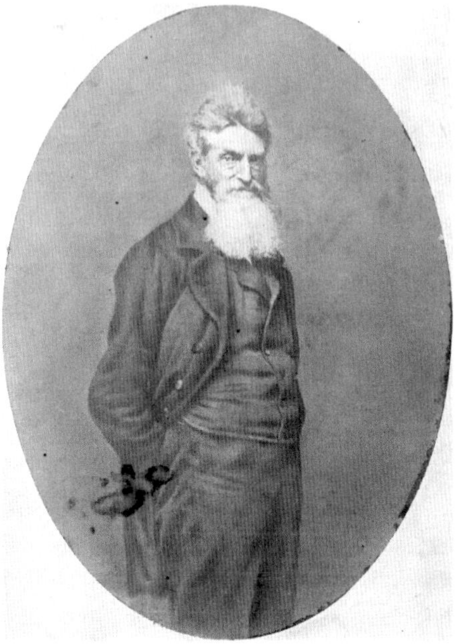

John Brown in 1859, shortly before his raid on Harpers Ferry. *Library of Congress.*

> *I was, however, a little disappointed with the appearance of the house and its location. After seeing the fine store I was prepared to see a fine residence in an eligible locality, but this conclusion was completely dispelled by actual observation. In fact, the house was neither commodious nor elegant, nor its situation desirable. It was a small wooden building on a back street, in a neighborhood chiefly occupied by laboring men and mechanics; respectable enough, to be sure, but not quite the place, I thought, where one would look for the residence of a flourishing and successful merchant.*

The interior of the house was even simpler. The Browns had decided to use their money to support fugitive slaves in Upstate New York rather than buying expensive furniture, so the inside of their home had "an air of plainness about it which almost suggested destitution," with "no sofas, no cushions, no carpets, no easy rocking chairs inviting to enervation or rest or repose." They ate a dinner of beef soup, cabbage and potatoes at a plain pine dinner table, which was "innocent of paint, veneering, varnish, or table-cloth."

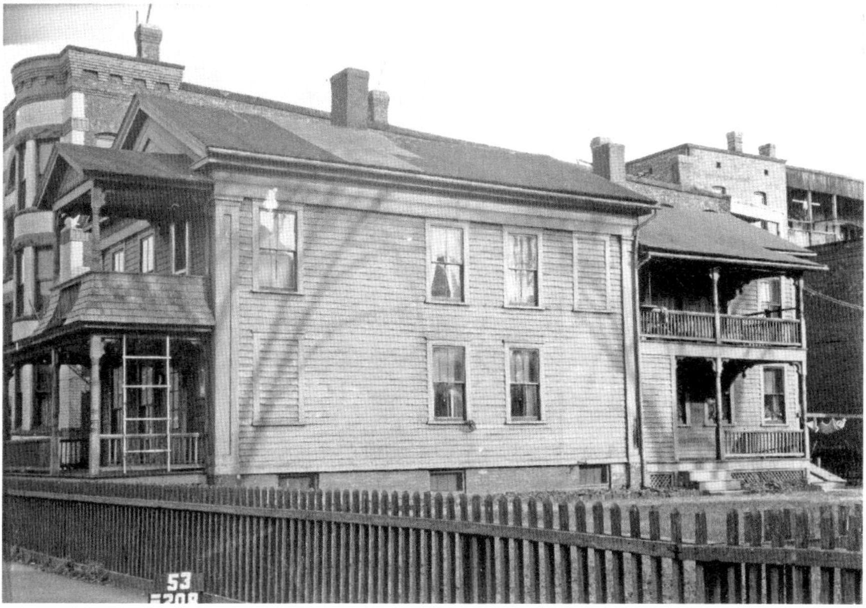


John Brown's house at 31 Franklin Street around 1938–39, nearly a century after he lived there. *Springfield Preservation Trust.*

At a time when it would not have been uncommon for a family like the Browns to hire servants, Douglass wrote that "mother, daughters, and sons did the serving, and did it well. They were evidently used to it, and had no thought of any impropriety or degradation in being their own servants." Like the house itself, he wrote, the family had "no disguises, no illusions, no make-believes."

At this point in his life, John Brown had already formulated a plan for overthrowing slavery, and after dinner, he described his ideas to Douglass. His plan called for small groups of well-armed men who would hide throughout the Appalachians, encouraging local slaves to run away and assisting them on their way north. He did not want a general slave rebellion but was not at all reluctant to shed blood or, if necessary, die in the process, with Douglass writing that Brown believed he "had no better use for his life than to lay it down in the cause of the slave." Up until this point, Frederick Douglass had been hopeful that slavery could be ended without violence, but he noted that, after this meeting with John Brown, "I became all the same less hopeful of its peaceful abolition. My utterances became more and more tinged by the color of this man's strong impressions."

During his time in Springfield, John Brown made other important connections in the local abolitionist community. He attended Old First Church, where he listened to the preaching of staunch abolitionist Samuel Osgood, and he also spent time with the black community in Springfield, forming friendships with men like Thomas Thomas, a former slave whom he employed with his company and confided in regarding his plans for overthrowing slavery.

Probably in part because of his focus on the abolitionist cause, his business here in Springfield was ultimately unsuccessful. John Brown left Springfield by 1851, but not before establishing the League of Gileadites. It consisted of forty-four black men who were responsible for protecting runaway slaves from capture, with John Brown instructing them to use violence if necessary.

John Brown became increasingly radical after leaving Springfield, participating in the Bleeding Kansas violence between pro-slavery and anti-slavery factions. In 1859, he finally carried out the plans that he had been working on since Springfield. He led a force of twenty-one men to the federal armory at Harpers Ferry, with the goal of seizing it and distributing its weapons to slaves across the region.

Local militia forces and a group of marines led by Robert E. Lee successfully defended the armory, and John Brown was captured and later executed for treason. He was a polarizing figure, though, with southerners reviling him as a lunatic and a terrorist, while northern abolitionists viewed him as a martyr. In the short term, his plan had failed, but his attack ultimately helped lead to the Civil War and the subsequent abolition of slavery.

John Brown's old house at 31 Franklin Street outlived him by just over a century. Over the years, it continued to be used as a private residence, even as larger brick apartment buildings were built around it. The front of the building was altered at some point, replacing the original one-story porch with a two-story one and turning one of the second-floor windows into a door. Like so many other Springfield landmarks, the house was eventually demolished in the urban renewal projects of the 1960s, part of which involved the wholesale destruction of the entire North End between the railroad tracks and Memorial Square. Along with his house, the entire lower section of Franklin Street is gone, and the site of his house is now just south of Interstate 291, where Northgate Plaza is located.

# SOLYMAN MERRICK HOUSE

For the first two hundred years of Springfield's history, its residential development had been mostly confined to the Main Street corridor. However, as the city began to industrialize in the early nineteenth century, many of its wealthier residents began building houses on the hill overlooking the town, especially along Chestnut Street and the lower part of Maple Street.

One such resident was Solyman Merrick, a tool manufacturer. Merrick, whose first name is also spelled Solymon and Solomon in historical records, patented the first monkey wrench in 1835. He sold the patent to Stephen C. Bemis, whose tool company Bemis & Call made monkey wrenches in Springfield for many years, and in 1841, he moved into a new house on Maple Street, at the northeast corner of Union Street. That same year, he married his first wife, Henrietta Bliss, the daughter of prominent merchant Theodore Bliss. She died in 1845, and three years later, he married Anne Clapp.

By 1850, Merrick had sold his house to lawyer and future mayor Ansel Phelps. He and his wife and their young son William moved diagonally across the street to a new house, located at 104 Maple Street. Just as Merrick's invention of an adjustable wrench had revolutionized the tool industry, his new house had a similar effect on the city's architecture. Up until this point, most of the houses in the city were designed by local architects in Greek Revival styles that many critics found uninspiring. Josiah Gilbert Holland, along with criticizing the bland architecture of Springfield's public buildings in his 1856 city hall dedication speech, also remarked that, regarding the city's new, expensive mansions, "a common horse-block has just as many, and just the same, architectural ideas in it as may be found in a street full of such."

This began to change with Merrick's house. Completed in 1850, it was designed by Leopold Eidlitz, who later built the old city hall, and it was one of the first buildings in the city to have a nationally prominent architect. Eidlitz was born in Prague and later immigrated to the United States, where he studied under architect Richard Upjohn. His Italian villa design for Merrick's house was a vast departure from the common Greek Revival homes of the early nineteenth century, and in 1864, the *Springfield Republican* wrote that, until this house, "there was not a handsome private house built in Springfield." The newspaper went on to write:

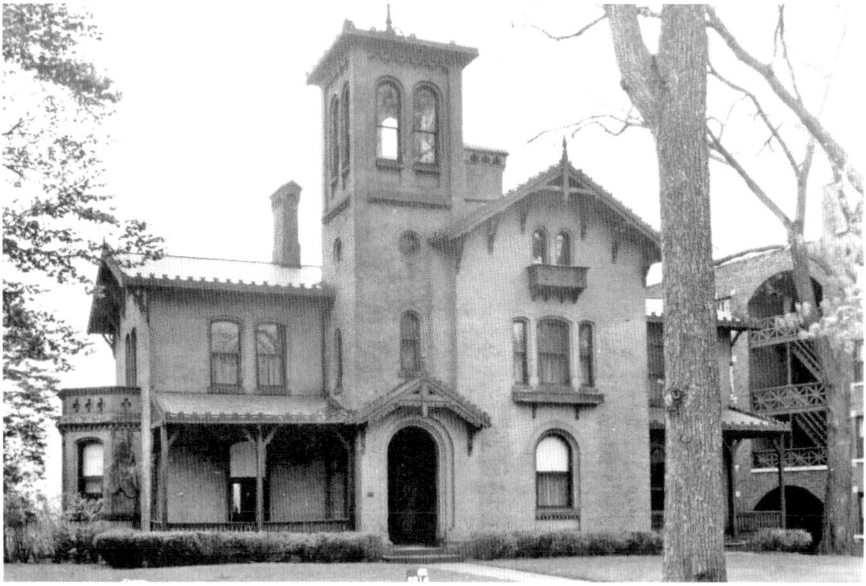

The Solyman Merrick House at 104 Maple Street, around 1938–39. *Springfield Preservation Trust.*

> *This was the work of a genuine architect. We remember distinctly the effect produced upon the public by this modest little structure. It was so different from anything around it—it produced such fresh and unusual ideas—that everybody quarreled with it, and nobody understood it. It has stood through a series of fifteen years, or so, and done its work. It has compelled people to admire it, and it is a question whether any structure has since been put up in the city, or designed for its various beautiful sites, that is its superior. It is a little architectural poem, exquisite in detail and exquisite as a whole.*

Merrick did not get to enjoy his new mansion for very long, though. He died in 1852, and his widow, Anne, continued to live here, along with her sister Caroline and Caroline's husband, Albert Briggs, who was mayor of Springfield from 1865 to 1867. Anne served as a nurse in the Tenth Regiment Massachusetts Volunteer Infantry during the Civil War, and her son William graduated from Harvard in 1870 and later became treasurer of the Springfield Gas Light Company, as well as the benefactor of Merrick Park at the corner of State and Chestnut Streets. William lived in the house until his death in 1887, and it was later owned by lumber dealer Frank C. Rice, who sold it in 1915 to Dr. Richard S. Benner, an obstetrician who remained there until his death in 1939.

Several examples of 1850s Italian villa architecture remain in the Springfield area, including the John Mills House on Crescent Hill and the Charles Ely House on Main Street in West Springfield, which was designed by Eidlitz's mentor Richard Upjohn. Solyman Merrick's old Greek Revival house at the corner of Maple and Union is also still standing, but his Italian villa at 104 Maple Street was demolished by the early 1960s and replaced with an office building that now stands on the site.

## BRIGHTWOOD

Today, Brightwood is a neighborhood in the northwest corner of Springfield, but its name comes from the home of Josiah Gilbert Holland, which once stood at 110 Atwater Terrace. Although virtually unknown today, Holland was a prominent writer and poet of the mid-nineteenth century. He was born in Belchertown, Massachusetts, in 1819, and after graduating from Berkshire Medical College in 1844, he moved to Springfield, where he practiced medicine for several years.

While in Springfield, he married Elizabeth Chapin, but he soon struggled in his career. He did not particularly enjoy being a physician, but he did like to write, so in 1847, he started publishing the weekly *Bay State Courier*. It lasted only six months, though, before he changed careers again and took a job teaching at a private school in Richmond, Virginia. At the time, northern teachers were in high demand in the South, and soon after, he was offered the position of superintendent in Vicksburg, Mississippi. The job was less prestigious than the title may suggest; Vicksburg's public schools were virtually nonexistent, but Holland worked to organize a school system based on what he learned in Massachusetts.

After a little over a year in Vicksburg, the Hollands returned to Springfield to care for Elizabeth's ailing mother, and Josiah was hired as an assistant editor of the *Springfield Republican*. Working under editor Samuel Bowles, he soon became a co-owner of the company, and his literary career flourished. His first major work was *History of Western Massachusetts*, which was originally printed in serial format in the *Republican* before being published as a two-volume book in 1855. Writing under his own name and under the pen name of Timothy Titcomb, Holland soon gained national recognition with works such as the long poem "Bitter Sweet" and a collection of essays titled *Titcomb's Letters to Young People, Single and Married*.

Holland had previously lived in a house on High Street, opposite where Wesson Memorial Hospital now stands, but in 1862, he used his new wealth to build his spacious Brightwood mansion. It was designed in the Swiss Chalet style and included a large central hall that was topped with a cupola and surrounded by the parlor, library, dining room, reception room on the first floor and five bedrooms and a nursery on the second floor. The house also had servants' quarters as well as modern luxuries such as indoor plumbing, but it was located on the outskirts of the city, reportedly prompting the question "Who ever would want to live there, except some harebrained poet like Dr. Holland?"

Harebrained or not, Holland lived here for five years and continued writing, including the long poem "Kathrina," which became one of his bestselling works. However, in 1867, he left Springfield, selling his share of the *Republican*, renting out Brightwood and taking a two-year vacation in Europe. When he returned to the United States, Holland moved to New York, where he became one of the founders and first editor of *Scribner's Monthly*.

He sold Brightwood to George C. Fisk, the president of Wason Manufacturing Company, who was building the company's new facilities in the Brightwood neighborhood. The Fisks had five children, three of whom died young, including eleven-year-old George Jr. and two-month-

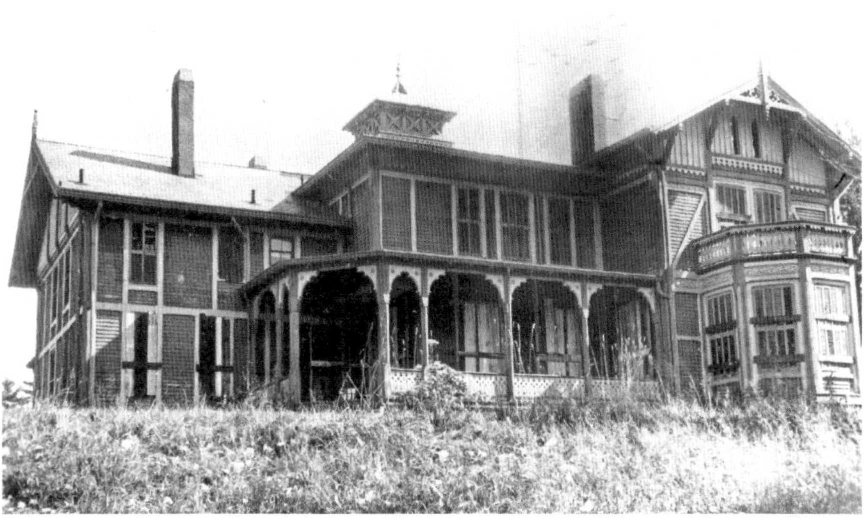

The west side of Brightwood, which once overlooked the Connecticut River, around 1938–39, a year or two before its demolition. *Springfield Preservation Trust.*

old Robert, who both died in 1879. Their only surviving daughter, Isabel, married Oliver Dickinson in 1888 in an elaborate ceremony at the house.

Isabel and Oliver lived at Brightwood with her parents, and their three children were born here. The house became even more crowded after Isabel's brother Charles died in 1904; his widow, Helene, moved in along with their three daughters, bringing the household up to eleven family members plus two servants.

George Fisk died in 1917 at the age of eighty-six, at which point the neighborhood was changing. Over fifty years earlier, the house had been far removed from the city, but by 1920, development had reached the area and much of the land around the house was parceled out for new houses. After her father's death, Isabel inherited Brightwood, and her son George moved into a house that he built on part of the property.

By 1930, the only family members still living here with Isabel and Oliver were their widowed daughter Julia and her daughter Catherine. Oliver died in 1931, and Julia inherited the house after Isabel's death in 1938. Brightwood had been the perfect mansion for a Gilded Age industrialist, but by the Great Depression, it was an economic burden for his surviving family members. It was far too large for just Julia and her daughter, so she sold the house, and it was demolished in January 1940.

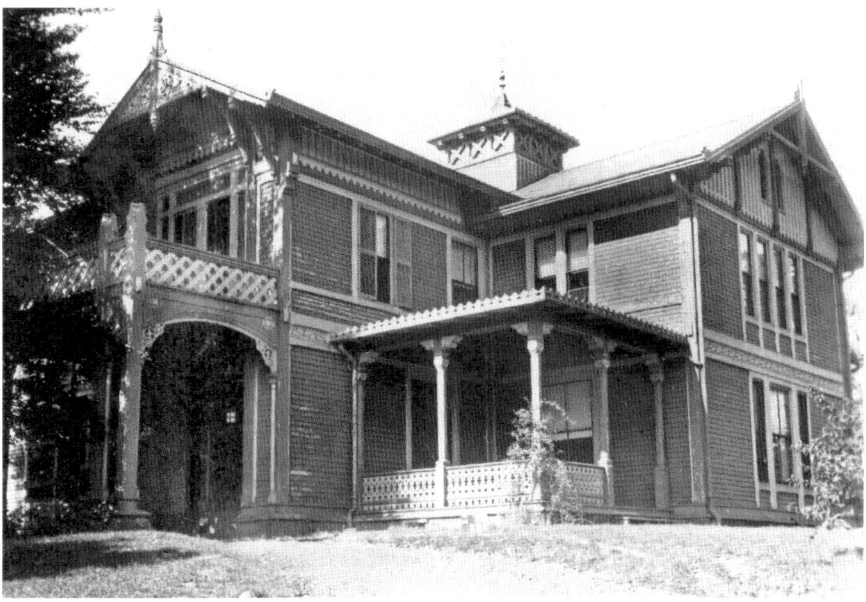

The east side of Brightwood, which faced Atwater Terrace, around 1938–39. *Springfield Preservation Trust.*

# TALCOTT HOUSE

Around the same time that Dr. Holland was building his house, other wealthy residents were eyeing Round Hill in the North End. Located in the triangular area between Main Street and Plainfield Street, this hill offered commanding views of the Connecticut River just like at Holland's Brightwood while being far closer to downtown Springfield.

One of Round Hill's early residents was Norman W. Talcott, an industrialist whose foundry specialized in making railroad car axles. The success of his business, which included contracts with a number of major railroads, enabled him to build his mansion here on Plainfield Street, overlooking Hampden Park and the Connecticut River. Its Gothic Revival design was praised by the *Springfield Republican*, which wrote that "the architectural elegance of the exterior is certainly excelled by that of no house in the vicinity, and reflects much credit upon the taste of the owner." The interior was equally impressive, with a parlor, dining room, library and reception room, along with ten bedrooms.

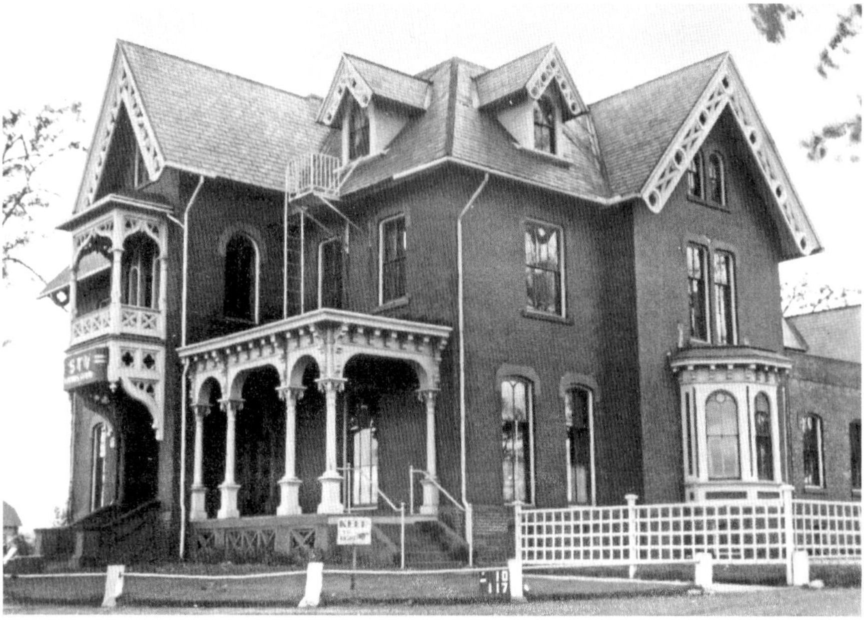

The Talcott House around 1938–39, during its time as the clubhouse for the Springfield Turnverein. *Springfield Preservation Trust.*

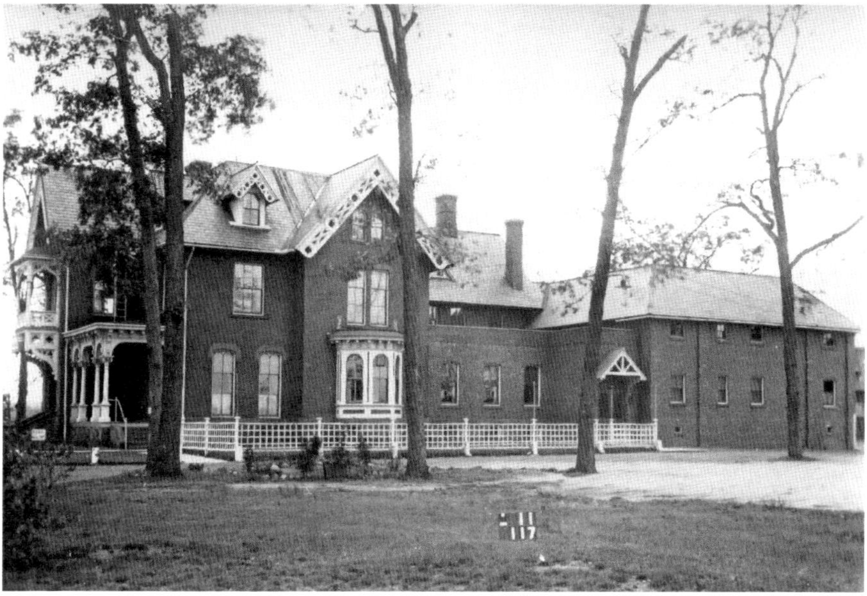

Side view of the Talcott House around 1938–39, showing the twentieth-century additions to the back of the building. *Springfield Preservation Trust.*

He moved into the house around 1868 along with his wife, Laura, and their daughters, Ella and Mary. Laura died in 1872, and two years later, Norman married Celia McKnight, the sister of the two men who were developing the McKnight district during this time. They lived here until his death in 1886, and the family later sold the property to liquor wholesaler Garrett S. Barry.

By the turn of the century, though, Round Hill was no longer as fashionable an address as it had been thirty years earlier, and the Barry family was the last to use the house as a residence. Garrett died in 1921 with no surviving children, leaving an estate valued at $400,000 and a will that was highly contested by extended family members.

The house was eventually sold after his wife's death in 1925, and it became the home of the Springfield Turnverein, a German American athletic and social club. The club remained there until 1966, when the historic house was demolished to build Interstate 91. Most of Round Hill was leveled by the construction of the highway and the ramps for exit 9, and the location of the house is now in the middle of the interchange, on the oval-shaped embankment between the highway and the exit ramp.

# ALLIS HOUSE

Along with Holland and Talcott, another leading citizen who built his house on the northern edges of the city was Waitstill H. Allis, a real estate developer and brick manufacturer. Allis came to Springfield in 1849 at the age of twenty-three and began his career in real estate. With the firm Hastings, Allis & Co., he purchased a farm in the North End and laid out Franklin and Congress Streets, between Main and Chestnut Streets.

The company parceled out the land, built houses and sold them, and to reduce construction costs, Allis opened a brickyard in 1852, which eventually employed two hundred men and produced twenty million bricks per year. Along with these houses, his bricks were also used for a number of buildings in Springfield, including some of the armory buildings, St. Michael's Cathedral, the old library and many schools and factories.

Allis never married, but in 1867, he built his mansion on Carew Street for him and his parents to live in. The central part of the Second Empire–style

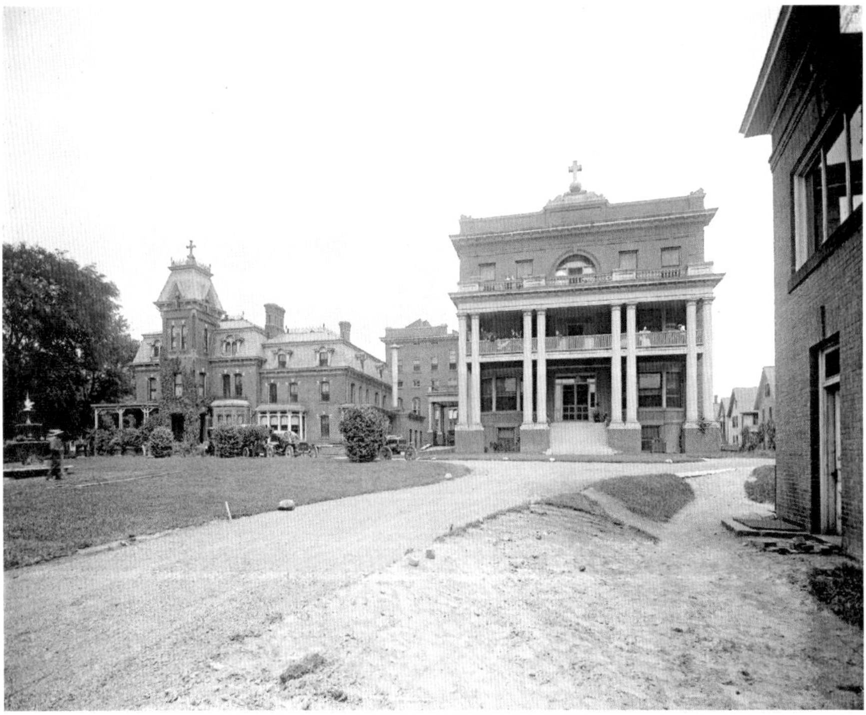

Mercy Hospital around 1900–10, with the original Allis House on the left. *Library of Congress.*

house was roughly square, with a large wing on the south side, a mansard roof and a tower above the main entrance. He, of course, built it out of brick, but he also used light-colored granite to provide contrasting colors above the windows and on parts of the tower.

Both of his parents died in the 1880s, and he sold the house in 1896. The Sisters of Providence converted it into the original Mercy Hospital building, with beds for thirty-five people, and they soon expanded the facility with a second building next to it. The old house was later used as a convent and a daycare as the hospital campus continued to grow, but it was last used in 2001 and fell into disrepair. Amid calls for its preservation, the hospital examined options for restoring the building, but administrators determined that it would not be feasible, so it was demolished in 2013 as part of a project to build a new medical office building.

## NATHAN BILL HOUSE

While some of Springfield's wealthiest citizens were building lavish homes in the North End, others chose the Ames Hill neighborhood along Maple Street. Situated over one hundred feet above downtown Springfield, this section of Maple Street had been home to prominent residents since the 1820s, when David Ames Jr. built his house here. However, development began in earnest after the Civil War, and by the 1870s, lumber dealer Jotham G. Chase was building a mansion here on the west side of Maple Street, nearly opposite Maple Court. The exterior was finished, but before he could complete the interior, he ran into financial difficulties, and the half-finished house sat empty until his death in 1884.

A few years later, the property was purchased by banker Andrew L. Fennessy. He sold the house itself, which was moved to a new location on Maple Court, and he proceeded to build his own house on the lot. The Shingle-style mansion was completed in 1888, but he did not live here long; within ten years, it was sold to Nathan D. Bill, who was living here by 1900 with his wife, Ruth, and their only child, fourteen-year-old Beatrice.

Bill made his fortune in the paper industry at a young age, and by the time he retired at the age of thirty-three, he was one of the city's wealthiest residents. He lived here on Maple Street for the rest of his life, during which time he played an active role as a civic leader and philanthropist.

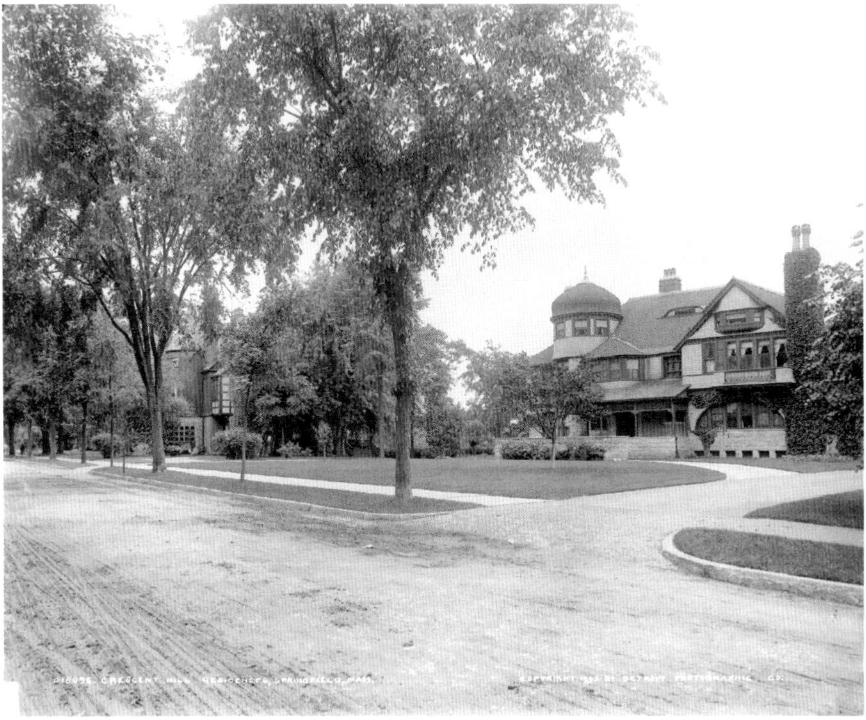

The home of Nathan Bill at 284 Maple Street, around 1905. *Library of Congress.*

Along with serving as a library trustee for sixty years, he was a member of the Park Board for twenty-eight years, where he both advocated for and contributed to the development of new city parks. This included donating land for five playgrounds across the city: Emerson Wight Playground, named for his father-in-law; Gurdon Bill Park, named for his father; Emily Bill Playground, named for his mother; Ruth Elizabeth Playground, named for his wife; and Nathan Bill Playground, which bears his name. He was also a strong opponent to the idea of building a golf course in Forest Park but instead gave some of the land needed to build the city-owned Franconia Golf Course.

After his death in 1947 at the age of ninety-one, many city leaders praised his contributions to Springfield, including former mayor J. Albin Anderson, who said, "Springfield is a finer city because Mr. Bill enriched it by his gifts and his spirit of unselfish giving." Another former mayor, Roger L. Putnam, named Bill as "one of the most public spirited men we have had," and Museum of Fine Arts director Frederick B. Robinson spoke of his "great generosity, sense of humanity and humility."

His mansion at 284 Maple Street, where he had lived for about fifty years, later became a nursing home. By the 1960s, it was vacant, but the owner planned to convert it and the carriage house into professional offices. However, the carriage house burned in a suspicious fire in 1967, and two years later, another fire destroyed the still-vacant mansion. The site of the house is still empty nearly fifty years later, with only the cracked pavement of the semicircular driveway left to mark where it once stood.

## DANIEL B. WESSON HOUSE

With the success of Smith & Wesson, it did not take long for Daniel B. Wesson to build an elegant house. He and his family moved into a new Italianate house on High Street in 1862, the same year that Josiah G. Holland moved out of his house across the street. The Wessons lived here for the next thirty-seven years, until the completion of their much larger house at the foot of High Street on Maple Street.

The Châteauesque mansion was designed by Bruce Price, a prominent architect whose works included the iconic Château Frontenac in Quebec City. It had a pink granite exterior, with twenty rooms inside that were lavishly decorated with wainscoting, carved oak and mahogany, tapestries, frescoes and marble fireplaces in every room. It also included modern conveniences such as hot water, gas and electric lighting and even a hydraulic elevator.

No house better exemplified the Gilded Age in Springfield than this house did. In an era that saw the construction of many fine houses in the city, Wesson's was the most expensive and also one of the shortest-lived as a residence. Both Daniel and his wife, Cynthia, died in the summer of 1906, just over two weeks apart, and the house, valued at $1 million, was inherited by their three surviving children. They all had houses of their own, though, including their eldest child, Walter, who lived farther up Maple Street next to Nathan Bill.

The house almost went to the Connecticut Valley Historical Society, who hoped to use it as a museum to house their collections. The Wesson heirs were willing to donate the house, provided that the organization raised $100,000 for an endowment to fund its maintenance. Despite a $10,000 contribution from J.P. Morgan, though, they were unable to reach the goal, and the house was instead sold to the newly formed Colony Club in 1915.

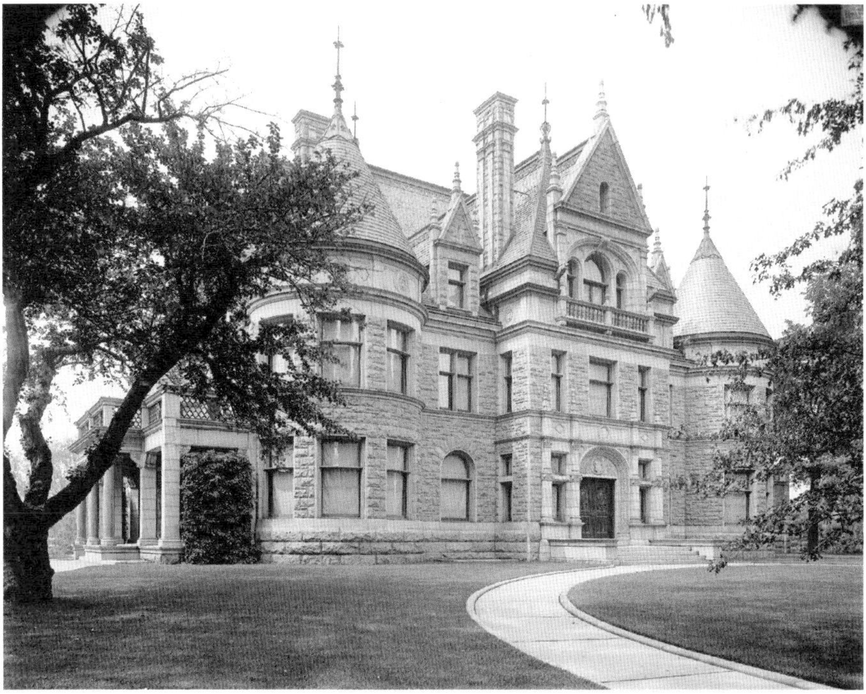

The home of Daniel B. Wesson at 50 Maple Street, around 1900–10. *Library of Congress.*

For the next fifty-one years the mansion was home to the club, and it saw visits from guests such as Presidents Taft, Coolidge, Hoover, Kennedy and both Theodore and Franklin Roosevelt, who attended the same event at the club in 1918. However, the building was destroyed in an early morning fire on February 20, 1966. The fire was likely aided by the extensive wood paneling, and it smoldered undetected until the heat inside caused an explosion that blew out the windows and doors. The approximately ninety firefighters who responded had to contend with not only the flames but also the sub-zero temperatures. Several sustained mild injuries, including Chief Edward C. Boyle, who told the *Springfield Union* the next day, "I feel like I got run over by a horse," after several sprains from falling on the ice.

It took over five hours to bring the fire under control, and by the time the sun rose in the morning, all that was left of the mansion was an ice-encrusted granite shell. The ruins were demolished, and the Colony Club spent several years in a temporary location before moving into their current home at Tower Square. The site at 50 Maple Street was rebuilt as an office building, and it now houses Baystate Visiting Nurse Association & Hospice.

# 7
# EDUCATION

The seventeenth-century Puritans of New England placed a strong value on education, and the early citizens of Springfield were no exception. In 1644, less than ten years after the town was settled, the town meeting delegated certain powers to the selectmen that included overseeing important functions such as "the Scouring of Ditches, & to the killing of wolves & to the training up of children in some good caling [*sic*]." In 1677, the town hired William Maddison as a schoolmaster, and he received three pence per week for every student he taught to read and four pence per week if he taught the student to read and write. Two years later, the town built its first schoolhouse, located west of Main Street on present-day Liberty Street, and by 1685, education was mandatory for all children between the ages of five and nine.

In the mid-nineteenth century, though, education had become a significant controversy. By the time it became a city in 1852, Springfield was divided into twelve different school districts, each of which taxed its own residents, employed its own teachers, set its own curriculum and maintained its own schoolhouse, with little oversight from the city government. Because of their authority to set policies, the districts tended to focus more on cutting taxes than on providing a good education, resulting in poorly funded schools across the city.

Springfield's population increase during the Civil War only magnified these problems, but under the leadership of Josiah Hooker, the school committee began to reform the city's schools. By 1870, the city's school system was divided into three years of primary school, six years of grammar school and four years of high school. The grammar schools were consolidated into five new buildings across the city, and in 1874, Springfield's new high school opened on State Street. Along with this, Springfield saw the establishment of new private schools, colleges, libraries and museums, all of which supplemented the growing city's educational system.

## HOOKER SCHOOL

The first of Josiah Hooker's proposed consolidated grammar schools opened on Main Street in the North End in 1865. It was named in his honor and designed by the Springfield-based architectural firm of Currier & Richards. The Italianate building was three stories tall, with a central clock tower facing Main Street, and in *King's Handbook of Springfield*, Superintendent Admiral P. Stone described it as "the finest of the grammar-schools in exterior appearance." On the inside, the Hooker School was built with four classrooms on each of the first two floors, with two more on the third floor, along with the principal's office and a large hall. Outside, the school had a landscaped front entrance that was reserved for the exclusive use of teachers and visitors, and in the back were two playgrounds separated by a tall fence, with one for boys and one for girls.

In describing the building shortly before it opened, the *Springfield Republican* reflected on the recent controversy about consolidating schools and increasing spending, referring to the "seething, vexatious delay," because of the fact that "the need of new houses was apparent and acknowledged, but not for three years could men be found with courage enough to meet the question and vote the necessary appropriations." The members of the city council who finally voted to build the Hooker School and the other grammar schools, the newspaper declared, "deserve as lasting gratitude as a people ever bestow on their rulers for their good deeds."

Under Josiah Hooker's reforms, each grammar school received incoming students from the primary schools in their area and also supervised these primary schools, providing a level of accountability that was nonexistent a decade earlier. The Hooker School's territory covered Ward One, which included most of the city north of the Boston & Albany Railroad tracks and west of Indian Orchard, and it had an enrollment of around five hundred students.

In 1867, the school committee published *Rules and Regulations of the Public Schools of the City of Springfield*, which established citywide standards for general

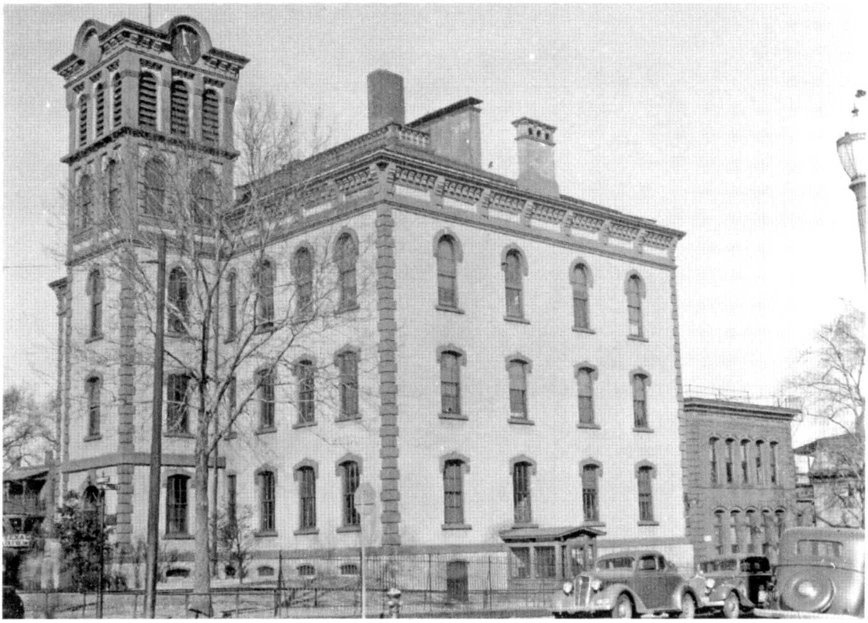

The Hooker School around 1938–39, during its time as the girls' division of the Trade School. *Springfield Preservation Trust.*

school procedures, the curriculum at each grade level, the responsibilities of teachers and the discipline of students. The school year was divided into three terms and began the first week of September and ended on the Friday before July 4. There were two sessions each school day, with the first from 9:00 a.m. to noon and the second from 2:00 p.m. to 5:00 p.m. Morning sessions began with a reading from the Bible and prayer, and each session had one twenty-minute recess period. Vaccinations were mandatory, and for any students who were unvaccinated or "infected with loathsome or contagious disease," it was "the duty of the teacher forthwith to exclude such children from the school." Students could not miss more than five school days per term, but a special ungraded school was established for students who were "irregular in their attendance." The Truant School was another option, for those convicted in police court of "truancy, idleness, vagrancy and other like misdemeanors."

The Hooker School building was damaged by a fire in 1875, but it was soon repaired. Later in the nineteenth century, it was expanded with an addition in the back and continued in use as a grammar school until 1918, when a new, larger Hooker School opened nearby. The old building sat vacant for a few years before being converted to use as the Continuation

School. Under state law at the time, children who worked needed to attend school at least four hours per week, so the Continuation School provided students with two hours of training in shop work and two hours of academic study each week.

The Continuation School closed in 1934 amid complaints that it provided students with few practical skills that prepared them for jobs, but the old building was soon put to new use as the girls' division of the city's rapidly growing Trade School. When it opened, the *Springfield Republican* noted that "the oldest and probably the dingiest" school building in the city was housing Springfield's "newest educational enterprise," but it seems only appropriate that the school building that brought transformation to Springfield's school system seventy years earlier would, near the end of its life, again play an innovative role in education.

The Trade School offered girls a choice of courses that included foods and clothing, trade dressmaking, power machine stitching and vocational homemaking. The students spent half of their time in the shops and half in academic classes, and unlike in the Continuation School, they were expected to attend for the entire school day.

In 1940, the city opened a new Springfield Trade School on State Street. It consolidated the girls' and boys' divisions into one school, later renamed in honor of Mayor Roger L. Putnam, who had established it during his time in office. The old Hooker School, now vacant again, was demolished in 1944. Over twenty years later, Interstate 291 was built over the site where the school once stood on the east side of Main Street.

## Chestnut Street School

The grammar schools established in the 1860s served the city well at the time, but by the 1890s, its population had doubled, and there was a pressing need for larger schools. This led to a significant investment in Springfield's public school system, with the city spending over $1 million between 1888 and 1904 to build new schools. In 1906, *Springfield Present and Prospective* noted that these schools were "recognized as among the best examples of school architecture in the country," and they included the Buckingham School, South Main Street School, Classical High School, Forest Park Middle School and the Chestnut Street School.

Completed in 1903, the Chestnut Street School was located at the corner of Chestnut and Prospect Streets in the North End. With twenty-one classrooms and forty-two desks in each room, it had a capacity of close to 900 students in grades five through nine. However, the significant growth in the neighborhood soon filled it beyond capacity, and six new classrooms were partitioned off in the hallways and the auditorium as enrollment grew to around 1,100.

Just five years after it opened, the school was expanded with a new wing to the south that nearly doubled its length along Chestnut Street. The original Classical Revival design of the school was duplicated for the addition, creating an essentially symmetrical façade that included two identical porticos, each with six massive limestone pillars. With the addition, the school had eleven new classrooms and a capacity of about 1,400, making it the largest grammar school in the state at the time.

The school continued to grow with subsequent additions in 1919 and 1928 and remained in use as a middle school for nearly one hundred years.

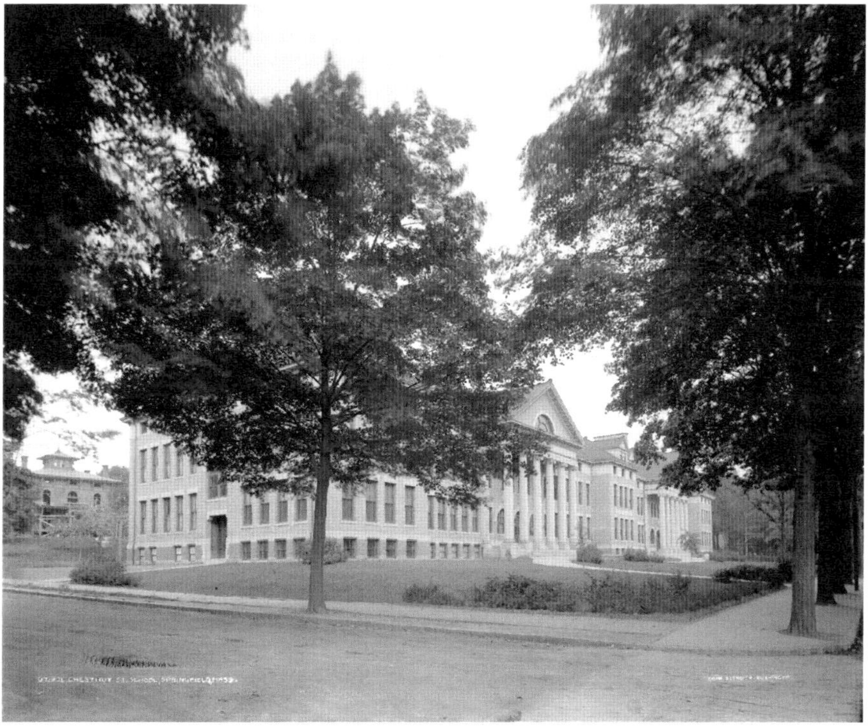

Chestnut Street School around 1908–15, with the original building in the foreground and the nearly identical addition in the distance. *Library of Congress.*

However, by the early 1990s, the school that had been described by the *Republican* in 1908 as "wonderful in its construction, equipment and facilities" was badly deteriorated. Years of deferred maintenance led to, as the same newspaper described it in 1995, "peeling paint, smelly bathrooms and bullet-riddled windows," with the nearly one thousand students occupying just the first two floors because the third floor had been condemned.

Some of the options for the school included either completely gutting the building and renovating it or demolishing it and rebuilding on the nearly four-acre site. Ultimately, though, a new school was built on a larger lot on Plainfield Street and opened in 1998 as Chestnut Accelerated Middle School. The old building was used by two of the city's alternative schools until 2004, when it finally closed amid what Mayor Charles Ryan described as its "indefensible and dangerous condition," which included some 691 code violations such as roof leaks, mold and structural problems. It remained vacant amid redevelopment proposals—such as converting it into housing units—none of which came to fruition. Finally, in September 2013, it was destroyed by arson, and the remains of the building were demolished the following spring.

# TECHNICAL HIGH SCHOOL

During the post–Civil War educational reforms in Springfield, the city's new high school was built on State Street, where Classical High School now stands. At the time, a high school education was not as universal as it would become in the twentieth century; in 1883, for example, the city's population was over 33,000, yet there were just 322 students enrolled in the high school, with a graduating class of just 46. The goal of the high school, as described in *King's Handbook*, was to prepare students "for college, for business, and for high intellectual culture."

In a rapidly industrializing city like Springfield, though, there was a demand for more than just college preparatory education. The variety of specialized industries in late nineteenth-century Springfield required skilled workers, and the city began to meet this demand as early as 1886, incorporating manual training into the grammar schools. The city boasted the first school district in the state to do so, and the educators' efforts were supplemented by the Springfield Industrial Institute. This private high school opened in the 1890s in the buildings at Winchester Square that would later become home to the Indian Motocycle Manufacturing Company. After the school closed in 1898, the city leased the buildings and established the Mechanical Arts High School as its first public technical high school.

After eight years at Winchester Square, the school moved into its permanent facility on Elliot Street and changed its name to the Springfield Technical High School. When the building opened in the fall of 1906, it was hailed by the *Springfield Republican* as "a crowning dignity to the city," that would make Springfield "a center of interest for educators and economists the country over." At a time when many school districts were struggling to provide adequate technical training, the completion of this building signified that the city "has shown itself to be equally in the front among educational centers of the country."

The school building was later expanded several times, but even when it was first completed, it was a substantial structure. Designed by Springfield's prominent father-and-son architectural firm of Eugene and George Gardner, the school had three stories, with a Renaissance Revival–style exterior of red brick and limestone. It was roughly T-shaped, with the main façade along

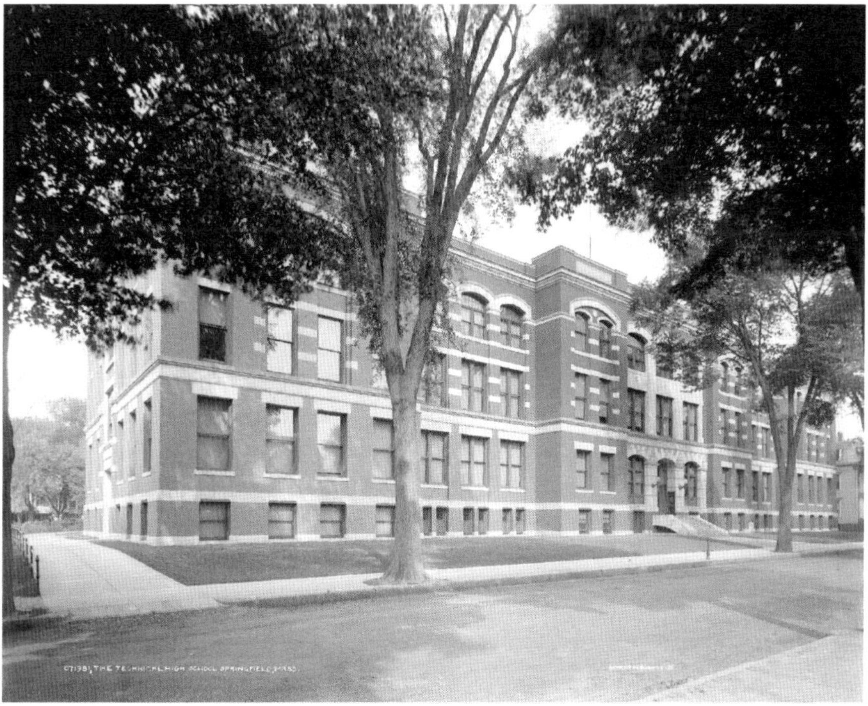

The Technical High School from Elliot Street, around 1906–15. *Library of Congress.*

Elliot Street. This side of the building housed the administrative offices and academic classrooms, and the shops were located in the rest of the building, along with a gymnasium and a seven-hundred-seat auditorium.

This new school had a capacity of nine hundred students, who could choose from one of three courses of study. Each option had substantial academic requirements in addition to the technical training but varied depending on the student's post-graduation goals. The first course was designed to prepare students for attending a technical or scientific college, with some schools even giving college credit for work done in the high school shops. The second course was a general scientific program that included all of the classes of a traditional high school, plus work in technical drawing and mechanical arts. The third course was for, as the *Republican* described it, "boys who are not able to do the literary and mathematical work demanded by the other two courses." This option focused more on shop work than on academics, with the intention of preparing students for a trade instead of college.

The school outgrew the original building in less than twenty years, and in 1924, three new buildings were added, extending the campus across the width of the block between Elliot and Spring Streets. One of the buildings added seventy-two new classrooms, and another was used by the Springfield

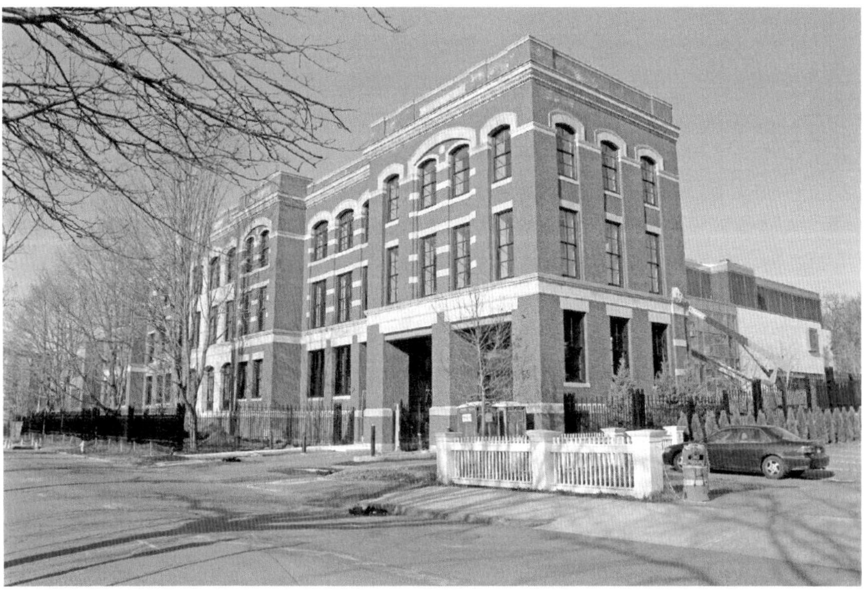

The surviving façade of the Technical High School, with the new data center building behind it. *Author's collection.*

Trade School until its own facility on State Street was completed in 1940. The last major addition to the Technical High School came in 1935, with a wing that included a 1,260-seat auditorium and two gymnasiums.

By the 1970s, the once state-of-the-art school was largely obsolete, and with the opening of Central High School in 1986, both the Technical High School and the nearby Classical High School were closed. In its eighty years in existence, Technical High had around thirty thousand graduates, among them hall of fame baseball player Walter "Rabbit" Maranville and Congressman Richard Neal.

Following its closure, the historic Classical High School building was converted into condominiums, but similar plans for the Technical High School building never materialized. The building stood vacant for years. Most of it was demolished in 2003 to make room for the new federal courthouse, leaving only the original section along Elliot Street. The rest—except for the façade of the building, which was incorporated into a new structure—was demolished in 2011 to build a state data center. Completed in 2013, it serves as a backup facility for the state's electronic records, playing a technological role that far exceeds anything that the school's founders could have imagined when it first opened in 1906.

## OLD CITY LIBRARY

The earliest recorded library in the city was called the Springfield Library Company, and it existed as early as 1796, when it had a collection of some 320 books. Several other libraries were established in the early nineteenth century, including the Franklin Library Association, which was made up of workers at the armory, along with the Hampden Mechanics' Association's library, the Young Men's Institute and the Young Men's Literary Association. None of these were true public libraries, though. Their privately owned collections were generally small, and only members had access to the books.

Although ubiquitous today, public libraries were virtually unknown prior to the mid-nineteenth century. Boston's public library, established in 1852, was among the first, but it did not take too long for the sentiment to catch on in Springfield. Just three years later, around 1,200 residents signed a petition asking for $2,000 to start a public library. The city council, mindful of the cost of the newly completed city hall, rejected the idea, but its proponents were undeterred, and in 1857, the collections of the Young Men's Institute and the Young Men's Literary Association were combined to form the City Library Association.

This quasi-public library was not initially funded with taxpayer money but through voluntary donations; proponents quickly raised about $8,000. The library moved into a room in city hall in 1859 and was open in the afternoon and evening every Tuesday and Friday. Aside from providing the space, though, the city still did not contribute any funds to the library, and its holdings remained small. That same year, the *Springfield Republican* noted that "the present condition of the library affords a very meager opportunity for supplying the wants of the readers." The paper illustrated the public benefits that would come from a larger, publicly funded library, arguing:

> [T]*here is little doubt that a more general habit of reading would be established among all classes of our citizens, which would tend greatly to furnish the mind with valuable information, in addition to the influence it would have in affording a pleasant occupation to our young people, who now are forced to contrive worse methods of spending their time.*

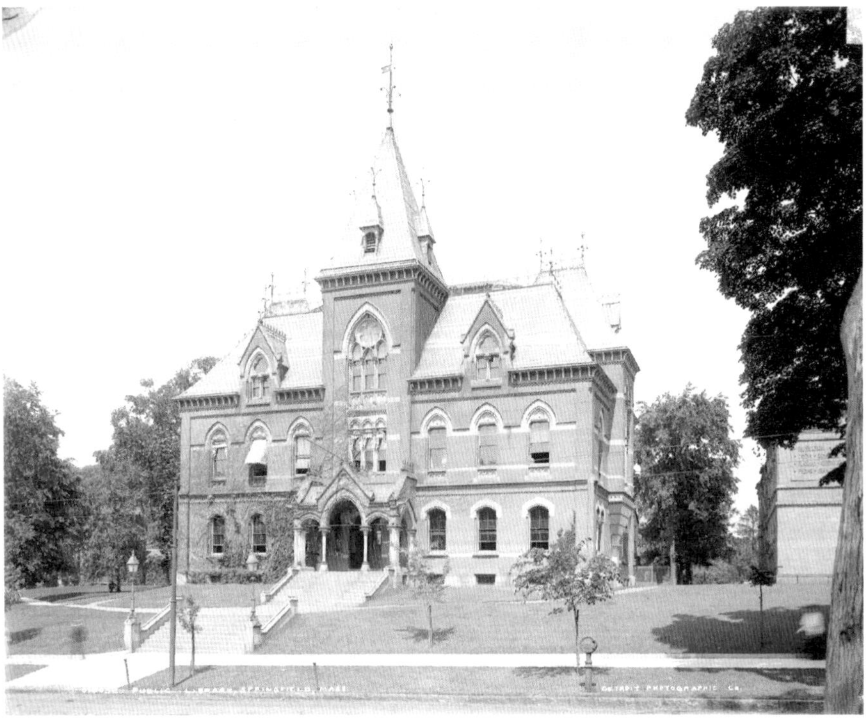

The old city library from State Street, around 1900–05. *Library of Congress.*

The city began funding the library in 1864, at which point it had grown to around seventeen thousand books in its now-overflowing space in city hall. With the library badly in need of a permanent home, George Bliss donated a parcel of land along State Street, plus $10,000 toward the construction of the building. The library association soon raised the rest of the money for it, and the new library building opened in 1871.

The brick Gothic Revival building was designed by New York architect George Hathorne, and when it opened it housed around 31,400 books. *King's Handbook* provides a description of the interior about thirteen years after it opened:

> *The main library-room proper is in the upper story, is domed, and, midway of its height, has a gallery extending completely round its walls, accessible by spiral iron staircases. Below the library-room, one entering from State Street finds, on his right, the museum; on his left, the reading-room, supplied with a good list of daily and weekly newspapers, magazines, and reviews, and furnished with every convenience and comfort, for the free use of all persons.*

At the time, the library was open every day of the week except Sundays, during which time any library resources could be freely used within the building. Borrowing books required a one-dollar annual subscription, which allowed an individual to take up to two books at a time. This nominal fee was dropped altogether for city residents in 1885, and by the turn of the century, patrons were allowed to borrow one fiction book at a time, plus a "reasonable number" of other books. By this point, the library even had a delivery service which, for eight and one-third cents per week, would bring books to subscribers at their home.

The building was later named in honor of William Rice, who served as librarian from 1861 until his death in 1897. He oversaw the library's growth from a small collection of books in city hall to—only a few years after his death—around 136,000 books. In 1905, in sharp contrast to the *Republican*'s early assessment of the library in 1859, *Springfield Present and Prospective* noted that:

> *No city in the country the size of Springfield has a public library collection approaching it in value. Few cities of any size take so genuine a pride or so active an interest in their library, contribute for its support from both public and private sources so generously, and in return expect and enjoy so large a use of its treasures.*

By this point, the library had added two additional buildings, with one serving as an art museum and the other a museum of natural history. Both of these structures are still standing as part of the Quadrangle, but the library itself was becoming too crowded for its growing collections.

Much of the funding for the first library building had been provided by local donors, but its replacement was built largely thanks to the efforts of Andrew Carnegie. The steel magnate was one of the wealthiest people in history, accumulating a vast fortune in the late nineteenth century before spending the rest of his life giving almost all of it away. Carnegie placed a high value on education and gave money to build 2,509 libraries around the world, including a new Central Library and 3 branch libraries in Springfield.

Carnegie provided some $200,000 to build the new library, with Springfield residents donating the remaining $155,000, but the old library still needed to be kept open during construction. So, the massive brick structure was moved back about two hundred feet, and the new library was built on its former spot. Once it was completed, the 180,000 books and other materials were moved into the building via a gravity-powered cable car system. It consisted of two cars, each with a capacity of around 150 books, that were connected to a cable; as the fully loaded one descended, it pulled the empty one back up to the old building. The entire process took just eight days, and during this time, the library remained open to the public.

The new library building, which is still standing along State Street, opened in January 1912. Nathan Bill, in his capacity as library president, gave the opening remarks, which included reading a letter from Carnegie, who was unable to attend but wrote that "I remember my visit to Springfield with great pleasure. I hope everything will pass off to your entire satisfaction. Springfield deserves what I have done for it, as is shown by its appreciation."

Despite the considerable effort to move the old library building, it was not in its new location for very long. Only a few months after its replacement was dedicated, the old building was demolished, clearing the way for what would become the Quadrangle. Its namesake was not forgotten, though. Rice Hall, the large hall on the west side of the library that houses its nonfiction works, is named in honor of the nineteenth-century librarian whose name was once on the old building.

8

# RECREATION

Springfield is widely known as the birthplace of basketball, but the city's tradition of sports and recreation goes far beyond James Naismith's invention. One of the earliest references to sports in the city records dates back to 1664, when the selectmen were faced with the problem of "the great damage done to ye glass windowes in ye meeting house by childrens playing about ye meeting house." Glass being an expensive commodity at the time, they ordered that "if any persons children or others, shall be found playing at any sports about the meeting house, whereby ye glass windows therof may be endamaged, such persons shall be liable to a fine of 12d a peece for each tyme they shall be found soe playing."

At the time, there were no public parks, and there would not be a significant park system for several more centuries. By the late nineteenth century, though, the city would gain substantial parkland from benefactors such as Orrick Greenleaf, Everett Barney and Nathan Bill, who donated land for Forest Park and a number of other parks and playgrounds across the city.

Around the same time, Springfield saw the development of organized sports. Venues such as Hampden Park hosted bicycle racing, professional baseball and college football games, and the Connecticut River was used for yachting and boat racing. Later in the century, of course, Springfield was the site of the world's first basketball game, and this tradition lives on today with the Naismith Memorial Basketball Hall of Fame.

# HAMPDEN PARK

The city's primary sports venue of the nineteenth century was Hampden Park, located in the triangle of land just south of the North End Bridge, between the Connecticut River to the west and the railroad tracks to the east. It was opened in 1857 by the Hampden County Agricultural Society, which—four years earlier—had sponsored the nation's first horse show at Federal Square next to the armory. Using the profits from the successful show, the organization purchased the land for Hampden Park.

The park was inaugurated in the fall of 1857 with another horse show. It was the nineteenth-century version of the Big E, and it attracted some twelve thousand people for the opening ceremonies. The event started with a parade from city hall to the park and included an opening prayer by the recently retired Reverend Samuel Osgood, a hymn written by Josiah Gilbert Holland and a keynote speech by prominent pastor and abolitionist Henry Ward Beecher, the younger brother of Harriet Beecher Stowe.

In his remarks, Beecher mentioned how some people thought it was not appropriate for him to participate in such an event where a prayer, hymn and sermon would be followed by a horse race. However, as the *Republican* described it, "he did not believe in letting the devil have all the best horses, as he was said to have the best music." Beecher warned against using the park for gambling, hoping that it would instead be used for "the development and

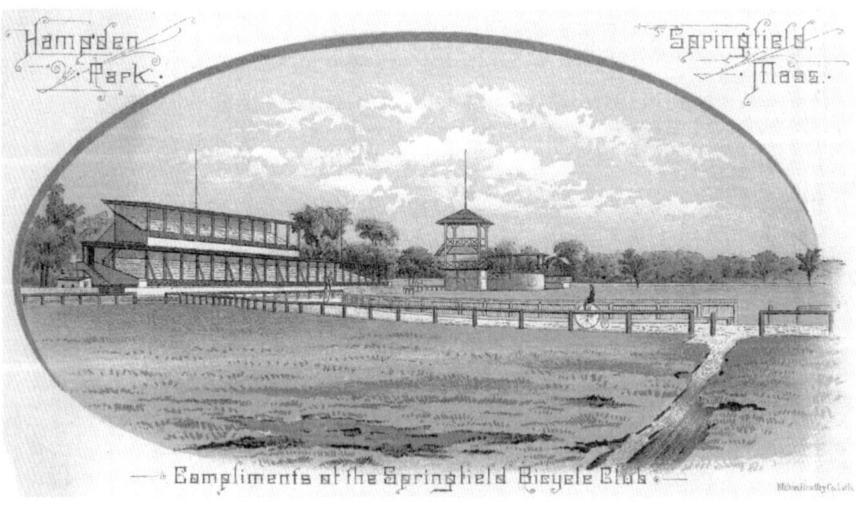


An 1891 lithograph of Hampden Park, with two bicyclists riding on the track. *Author's collection.*

perfection of the noblest animal of all." His speech was well received by the crowd, who "interrupted from first to last [with] cheers and bursts of mirth," and after he "sat down amid great applause," the ceremony concluded with a speech by Mayor Ansel Phelps and a closing hymn.

Aside from horse shows, Hampden Park soon saw other uses. At the start of the Civil War, the Tenth Regiment Massachusetts Volunteer Infantry mustered here. The soldiers, who were primarily from western Massachusetts, began arriving in May 1861 and camped here until July, when they headed south to join the war.

After the war, baseball became a popular pastime across the country, and here in Springfield, Hampden Park became the city's center of baseball activity. In 1869, baseball's first openly professional team, the Cincinnati Red Stockings, played here against the amateur Springfield Mutuals team. The Red Stockings were in the midst of a perfect 65-0 season and an 84-game winning streak, and they completely overmatched the hapless Mutuals, who lost by a score of 80–5 in what the *Republican* described as a "frightful castigation of our Springfield boys."

The first professional baseball league, the National Association, was established two years later, and although Springfield never fielded a major-league team of its own, several games were played here in the 1870s. In 1872, the Harvard-Yale Regatta was held on the Connecticut River in Springfield, and part of the festivities included a game between the Troy Haymakers and the Middletown Mansfields. Troy won 7–0, but Middletown's team included rookie Jim O'Rourke, a future hall-of-fame catcher who played major-league and minor-league baseball until his retirement in 1912 at the age of sixty-two.

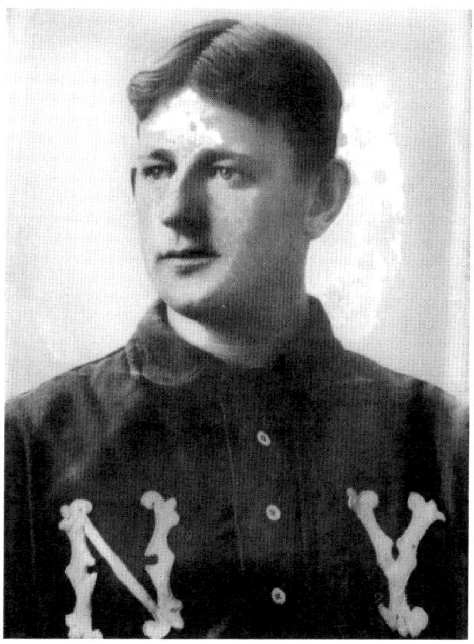


A 1904 photograph of Jack Chesbro, who played his first professional game for Springfield in 1895. *Library of Congress.*

The regatta was held in Springfield again in 1873, and nearly 2,500 spectators watched the Boston Red Stockings defeat the Philadelphia Athletics 21–13 at Hampden Park. The Red Stockings, who later became the Boston Braves, Milwaukee Braves and now the Atlanta Braves, played one more game here on May 14, 1875. Proclaimed in advertisements as a "Great Championship Game of Base-Ball," the spectators who paid the fifty-cents admission watched the Boston Red Stockings defeat the Washington Nationals 13–1, en route to a 71-8 season and its fourth consecutive league championship.

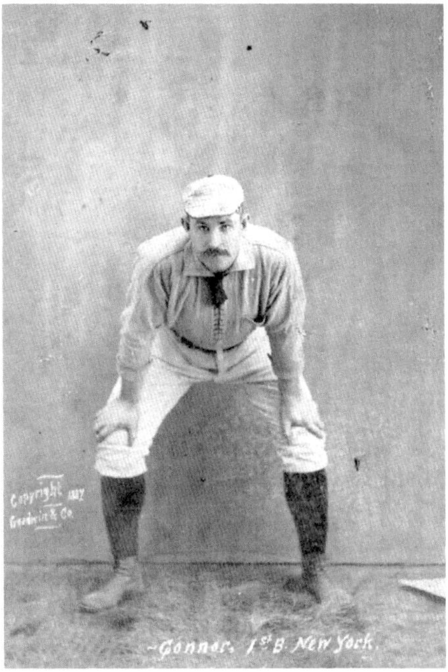

An 1888–89 baseball card of hall-of-fame first baseman Roger Connor, player-manager of the Springfield Ponies in 1902 and 1903. *Library of Congress.*

Springfield gained a professional baseball team of its own in 1878, with a minor-league team from the International Association. The city had several more teams throughout the 1880s, but minor-league baseball did not become well established here until 1893, when the Springfield Horsemen began playing at Hampden Park. Later named the Ponies, the team enjoyed some early success, including winning the Eastern League championship in 1895.

During Springfield's time as a minor-league city, Hampden Park was the home field of a number of prominent baseball players. Hall-of-fame pitcher Jack Chesbro, who is best known for winning forty-one games in 1904 to set a modern major-league record, played his first professional game for Springfield in 1895. A few years later, hall-of-fame first baseman Roger Connor played his last professional game here while serving as player-manager in 1902 and 1903. During his major-league career from 1880 to 1897, he hit 138 home runs, which was an all-time record that was not broken until Babe Ruth reached it in 1921. One of Connor's players on the 1903 team was Jim O'Rourke, who had first appeared in Springfield with the Middletown Mansfields in 1872. He had also played here as a member of the Red Stockings in the 1873 and 1875 games, and he would return to Springfield one last time in 1907 as a fifty-six-year-old player for the Ponies. Other hall of famers who played for Springfield included first baseman Dan

Brouthers, who played here from 1896 to 1899, and outfielder Hugh Duffy, who played here in 1887 and went on to become a star player in Boston, setting an all-time record .440 batting average in his 1894 season.

During this time, Hampden Park was also used for bicycle racing. The first major race here was in 1882, attracting around twelve thousand people. Fifteen-year-old George Hendee won the half-mile race, with a time of 1:25 on his penny-farthing bicycle. The next year, more than twice as many people attended the three-day event at the park, and this time, Hendee won the twenty-mile amateur race with a time of 1:07:32, beating both the American amateur and professional records for the event. Hendee would go on to achieve national prominence in bicycle racing, entering 309 races and winning all but 7 of them. After his retirement from the sport, he would go on to achieve greater fame in Springfield as the founder of the Indian Motocycle Manufacturing Company.

Along with baseball and bicycling, Hampden Park was also the site of major college football games. From 1889 to 1894, the Harvard-Yale game was held here—on neutral ground between Cambridge and New Haven—and it produced some memorable moments in football history. During the 1892 game, Harvard introduced the Flying Wedge formation, a play that was as effective as it was dangerous. At the time, forward passes were illegal, so to advance the ball Harvard borrowed an ancient military tactic. The offensive players arranged themselves in a V formation, locked arms and charged at the defensive line, concentrating the momentum of all eleven players on a single helpless defender. The play caught on across college football, but it caused so many injuries that it was banned just two years later.

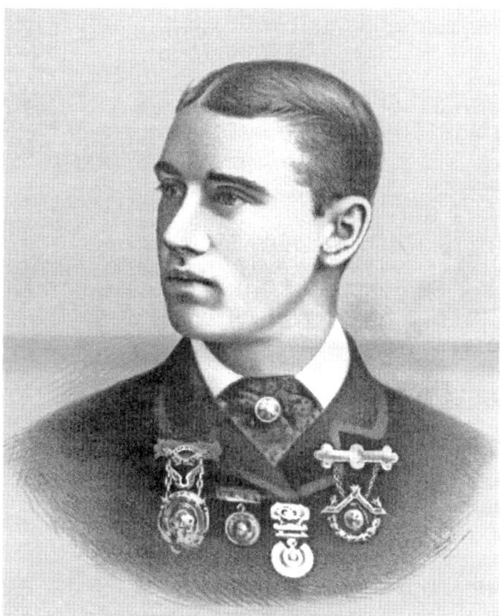

An 1884 print of George M. Hendee, the "Champion Amateur Bicyclist of America." *Library of Congress.*

Despite this rule change, though, the 1894 Harvard-Yale game was particularly brutal. Both teams were undefeated going into the game on the second-to-last week of the season, and the rivalry brought some twenty-three thousand fans to Hampden Park. Players at the time were expected to play both offense and defense for the whole game, and neither side wore much protective equipment; most of Yale's players wore nose masks and earflaps, while Harvard made do with just shin guards. The result was later referred to as the "Hampden Park Blood Bath" and the "Springfield Massacre." Six players were taken off the field with injuries, and two others were ejected from the game for unnecessary roughness. The next day, the *Springfield Republican* described the park as being like "the arena of a Roman amphitheater," and the second half of the game in particular was "a desperate and long-drawn-out struggle, full of gore and carnage, with surgeons running on and off the field after every other play."

The most serious of these injuries was to Yale's star right tackle Fred Murphy. During the first half, he was "knocked senseless" in a violent collision, and although he remained in the game, he was so disoriented that before each play his teammates had to remind him which direction to run. Clearly suffering from a concussion, he attempted to continue playing before being knocked unconscious early in the second half. He was taken off the field in a stretcher and brought to Springfield Hospital, where he lay comatose for several hours before eventually recovering. Other Yale injuries included Alexander Jerrems with a sprained knee, and Frank Butterworth, whose eye was badly gouged. Harvard also lost key players to injuries, starting with star halfback Charlie Brewer, who attempted to play through an injured ankle before having to be carried off the field. Later in the game, Bob Hallowell left with a broken nose and Edgar Wrightington with a dislocated collarbone caused by Yale captain Frank Hinkey, who tackled and jumped on him while Wrightington was making a fair catch.

Yale ultimately won, 12–4, but the game had a far greater effect beyond just the score. The resulting outrage from the game threatened the future of football, with many calling for it to be abolished. Ultimately, it helped to bring about changes that made the game safer, but Harvard and Yale did not play each other for the next two years. When they resumed their rivalry in 1897, the game was held in Cambridge, and since then, it has alternated locations between the home fields of Harvard and Yale, although Hampden Park continued to be used for other Ivy League football games into the early twentieth century.

Most of the old Hampden Park was demolished by 1908, when the Boston and Maine Railroad expanded its rail yard onto part of the site. A new baseball diamond was built on the northern part of the grounds near the North End Bridge, and although its exact location and orientation shifted several times over the years, this site remained the home of Springfield's minor-league baseball for nearly sixty years. First named League Park, it was later renamed Pynchon Park and home to the Springfield Ponies, Rifles, Nationals, Cubs and finally the Springfield Giants, until 1965. The Giants relocated to Waterbury for the 1966 season, and any hopes of returning baseball to the city were dashed in September 1966, when a fire destroyed Pynchon Park. The site of Hampden and Pynchon Parks is now an industrial and commercial development along Avocado Street, with nothing remaining from the venues that were once located here.

## FOREST PARK

Although nineteenth-century Springfield residents could enjoy Hampden Park as spectators, they still lacked public recreational facilities of their own. *King's Handbook* noted in 1884 that "Springfield possesses no large park for the use of its people" but mentioned several proposals that were being

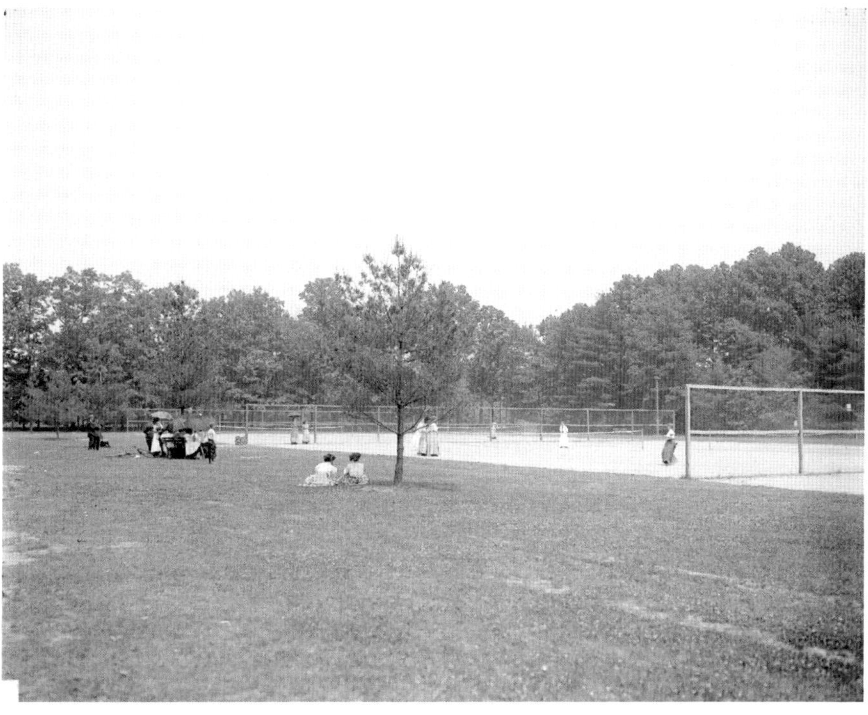

Women playing on the tennis courts at Forest Park, around 1900–10. *Library of Congress.*

considered at the time to provide the city with such a park. One option was to purchase the property along the riverfront in downtown, while another was the land around the Watershops Pond, which was still largely undeveloped at the time.

The riverfront park idea was favored by many, including Mayor Henry Phillips. The newly established park commission explored the idea of purchasing the nearly half mile of riverfront property between Bridge Street and Howard Street, which was valued at about $125,000. Before the city could take any action, though, in 1884, fellow park commissioner Orrick H. Greenleaf offered to donate around sixty-five acres of land in the southern part of the city. The land was accepted and named Forest Park, and by the end of the year, the city had purchased an additional twenty-five acres from other landowners for just $3,200.

The only problem with the new ninety-acre park was its distance from downtown. Located over a mile and a half from Court Square, it was in a sparsely developed residential area with no trolley lines connecting it to the city. In the early years, the city worked to develop the park with roads, bridges and a pavilion, but it remained underutilized by residents until 1890, when the Springfield Street Railway opened a trolley line to the park. The line formed a triangle along Fort Pleasant, Sumner and Belmont Avenues around the new Forest Park neighborhood, which was becoming one of the city's most desirable residential areas.

That same year, the park grew with additional donations, the largest of which came from Everett H. Barney. He was the owner of Barney & Berry, a Springfield company that manufactured ice skates, and in 1883, he had used his considerable wealth to build Pecousic Villa, a mansion overlooking the Connecticut River near the Longmeadow border. Along with the house, he had over one hundred acres of property, and he planned to build a house for his only child, George. However, George died in 1889 at the age of twenty-six, and instead of building his son a home on top of Laurel Hill, he built a mausoleum there.

A year after his son's death, Barney donated his property to the city, with the stipulation that he and his wife would be able to live here for the rest of their lives. With this donation, Forest Park extended all the way to the Connecticut River and incorporated Barney's well-landscaped property along with views of the river and downtown Springfield from atop Laurel Hill. When the gift was formally announced to the public, the *Springfield Republican* praised Barney's generosity, writing:

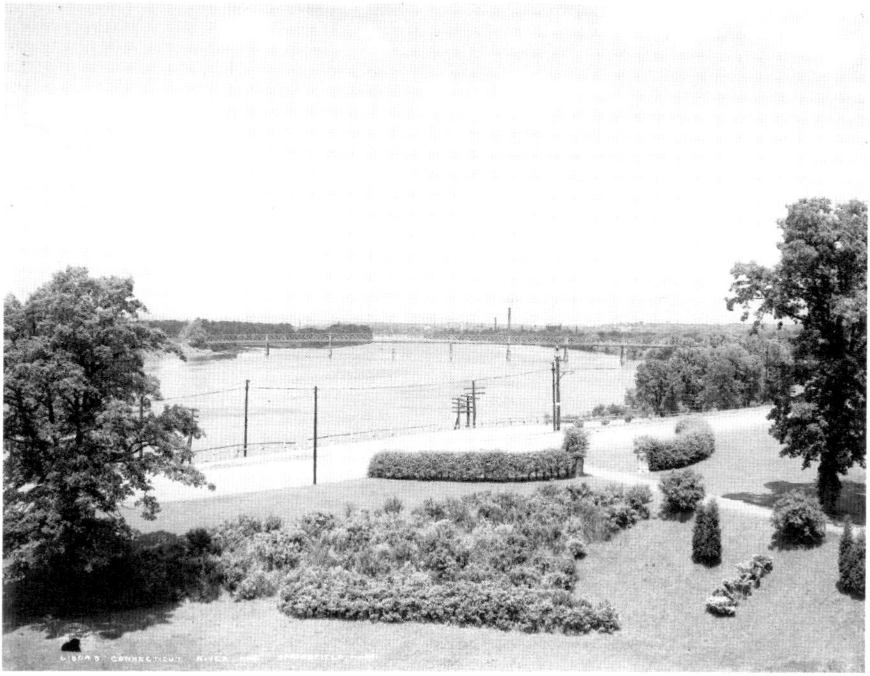

The view from the top of Laurel Hill around 1905, facing Springfield and the old South End Bridge. Interstate 91 now cuts through the foreground here. *Library of Congress.*

> *We are in due time to come into possession of an extensive estate, together with the fine buildings which have been erected thereon, and this acquisition, added to what we now possess, will give us a park that for beauty of situation and diversified features ought to satisfy the most exacting taste. The exceptional beauty of such a gift, when associated with the memory of a beloved son, will be recognized by everybody. Forest park will stand as a memorial of the Barneys, father and son, of Mr. Greenleaf and other contributors to the acres, during all the generations that are to come, contributing to the health and happiness of the people and making a feature of high value in the local life.*

As the newspaper predicted, Forest Park has been enjoyed by generations of Springfield residents ever since, but it has not been without some changes. Barney's wife, Eliza, died in 1905, and he died in 1916 at the age of eighty. They were buried with their son in the mausoleum on Laurel Hill, and the city took over the mansion. Starting in 1921, it was used as a venue for social events, and in 1944, it reopened as a museum, housing the Forest Park Museum of Natural History and the Barney Industrial Museum.

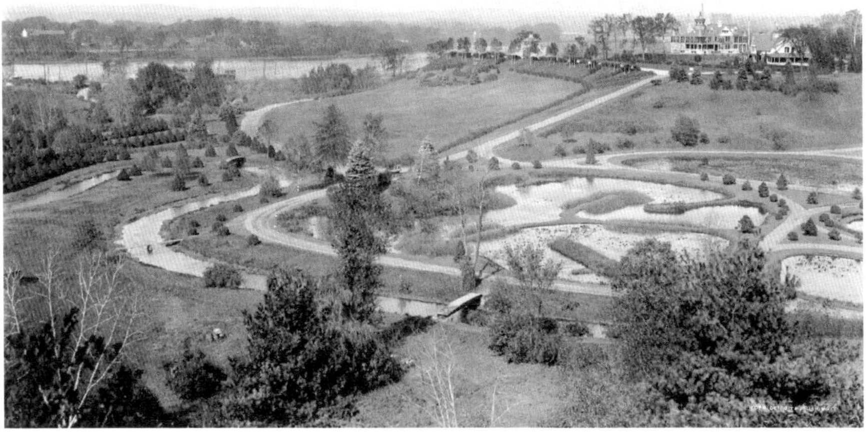

The view of the Barney estate around 1910–20, with the aquatic gardens in the foreground, Laurel Hill in the center and Pecousic Villa on the right. *Library of Congress.*

During his lifetime, Barney had many ideas for improving Springfield, including reconnecting the city to the Connecticut River waterfront. He lobbied for the removal of the railroad tracks along the river, which made it difficult to directly access the river from Forest Park. Writing a few days after his death, the *Republican* explained how he had hoped that "portion of the city could be redeemed from the neglect and unsightliness which had been permitted to overcome the large possibilities for betterment which he saw there."

The problem with Forest Park's location, though, was that there was nowhere else for the railroad tracks to go. The same hill that gave Pecousic Villa its commanding views also formed a transportation bottleneck, and all north–south traffic along the east side of the Connecticut River had to pass through the narrow space between the river on one side and hills on the other. As a result, the railroad tracks were never moved, and with transportation changes later in the twentieth century, the park not only was further isolated from the river but also lost its most prominent landmark.

In 1956, the *Springfield Union* reported that the museum at Pecousic Villa attracted around thirty thousand to forty-four thousand per year, with visitors from across the country and even overseas. However, less than three

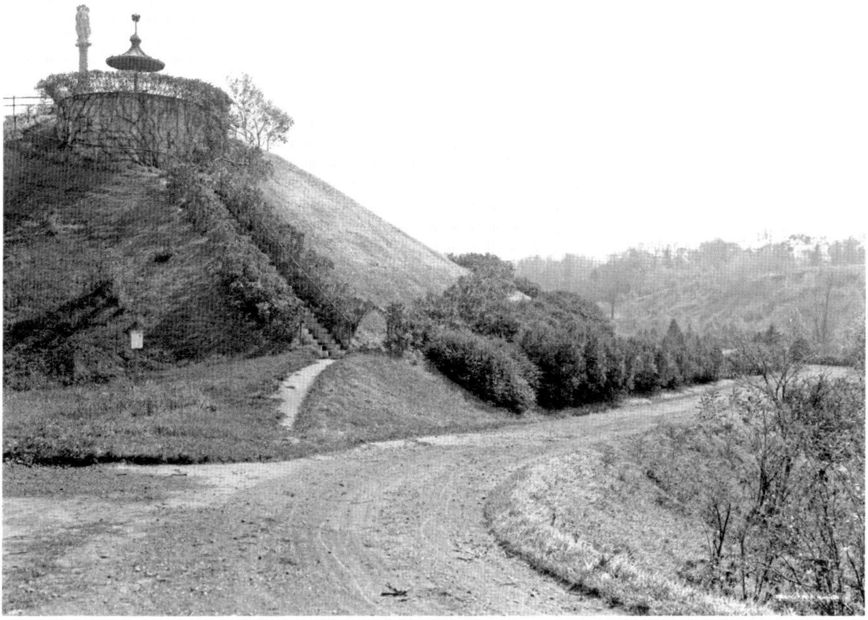

The base of Laurel Hill around 1910–20. The road here is now Interstate 91, but the overlook on the left is still visible from the highway. *Library of Congress.*

years later, the house stood in the way of the planned Interstate 91, and the same newspaper reported that "it is not an attraction of interest" and that "the esthetic value of the structure is negligible. Indeed, it is considered by many an architectural monstrosity." The park commission estimated that it would have cost over $150,000 to move the house, and it unanimously voted to demolish the house instead, believing that the money could be better spent in other ways. The *Union* agreed with the decision, writing that "the changing face of Springfield inevitably means breaking with the past," and Barney's mansion was demolished several months later.

One unusual twist came when the city solicited bids for its demolition. All of the contractors who submitted bids wanted several thousand dollars for the job, except for John Lizak of Palmer, who offered to *pay* the city ten dollars to demolish it, provided that he could keep the building materials. The park commission accepted his bid, and Lizak demolished the house while salvaging the stained-glass windows, mahogany woodwork and other valuable materials.

Interstate 91 now passes through the spot where Pecousic Villa once stood, and the only view from atop Laurel Hill today is that of a highway interchange. However, the rest of Forest Park continues to serve as a lasting legacy to Barney, Greenleaf and the other benefactors who gave the city its largest park. Now up to 736 acres, the park is used for a variety of recreational activities, and there are some remnants of the Barney estate. The aquatic gardens that he created are still maintained, the mausoleum still stands on top of Laurel Hill and, although Pecousic Villa is gone, its carriage house survived demolition and is now used for weddings and other private events.

## Birthplace of Basketball

One of Springfield's most significant contributions to the world has been the invention of basketball, which occurred in a nondescript brick building at Winchester Square that has long since been demolished. Most major sports do not have a distinct inventor or moment when they were invented; rather, sports like baseball, football and hockey evolved into the sports that we recognize today, often by incorporating rules from earlier games.

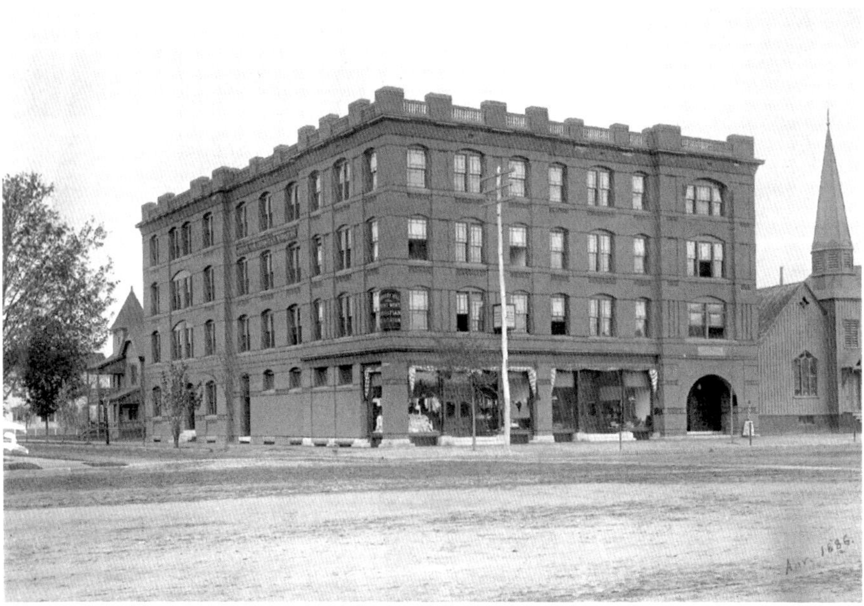

The School for Christian Workers building around 1886, where basketball was invented five years later. *Springfield College, Babson Library, Archives and Special Collections.*

Basketball, however, was the result of Springfield's population growth and prosperity in the second half of the nineteenth century. In 1885, David Allen Reed established the School for Christian Workers, for the purpose of training Sunday school superintendents and YMCA administrators. A year later, the school opened a four-story brick building on State Street, at the northeast corner of Sherman Street. The building included classrooms, dormitory rooms and, most significantly, a gymnasium.

The gymnasium reflected the YMCA's emphasis on physical education. The building's dedication exercises included a speech by William Faunce, the pastor of Springfield's State Street Baptist Church who would later serve as president of Brown University for thirty years. In his speech, Faunce spoke of the importance of the gymnasium, commenting on how, unlike those of the past who were "pale, attenuated, weak" Christian workers now "believe in cultivating a sound body for a sound mind, and I am glad to see here the well-furnished gymnasium."

The success of the YMCA program led to it becoming a separate institution in 1890, the International YMCA Training School. That same year, twenty-eight-year-old James Naismith entered the school as a graduate student. A Canadian native and graduate of McGill University and Presbyterian College in Montreal, Naismith had originally planned on becoming a pastor but decided that he could have a greater impact by working with young athletes through the YMCA. He entered the school's two-year program in the fall of 1890, joined by Amos Alonzo Stagg, a Yale graduate and All-American football player who had played in the Harvard-Yale game at Hampden Park a year earlier. Stagg shared Naismith's vision for using athletics as a way of ministering to young men, and he recruited Naismith to play on the school's new football team.

During his second year, Naismith was working as an instructor under Dr. Luther Gulick, the dean of the physical education department. At the time, the most popular sports were baseball and track in the spring and football in the fall, but in the winter, physical education students spent their time in the gymnasium, where they were largely limited to gymnastics and calisthenics. Late in 1891, Gulick asked Naismith to take over a particularly challenging physical education class of eighteen students. These students were already athletic and saw little value in the class, especially when they were limited to repetitive gymnastics and contrived, childlike indoor games. So, Naismith's challenge was to come up with a game that they would enjoy.

He knew he needed a game that would be competitive in order to hold their interest, but it also had to be practical in the school's sixty- by thirty-foot gymnasium. First, he tried to modify existing sports, including football, soccer and lacrosse, but these failed. Even with modifications, they were dangerous to both the participants and equipment, and the students were reluctant to accept what they saw as watered-down versions of their favorite sports. What he needed instead was a completely new game.

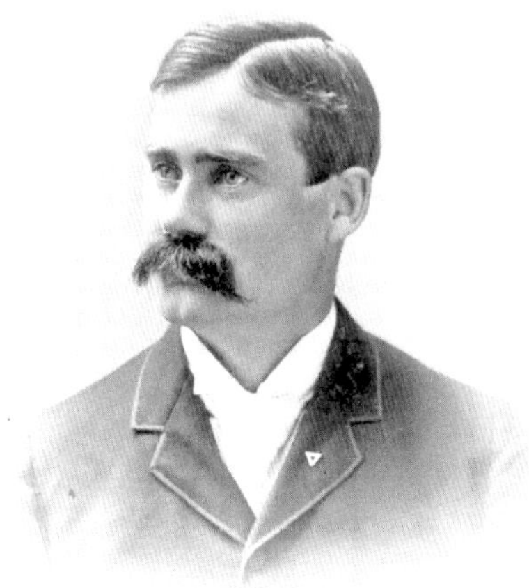

James Naismith around 1893, during his time as a faculty member at the YMCA Training School. *Springfield College, Babson Library, Archives and Special Collections.*

Naismith realized that, for a game to be safely played by eighteen people in a confined space, it would need to have limited physical contact between players, which meant players could not run with the ball. It also needed a way of scoring goals that emphasized accuracy over force, hence a horizontal goal that required a soft, arcing throw in order to score. The goal also needed to be above the heads of the players, so that the opposing team could not simply stand around it to block the ball.

The new game was simple, requiring no special equipment aside from a soccer ball and two goals, which Naismith originally envisioned as wooden boxes. The building's custodian had two empty peach baskets, though, so he used those instead, mounting them along the base of the gallery, ten feet above the gym floor. Along with this, he wrote thirteen rules for the game and posted them on a bulletin board for students as they arrived for class on December 21, 1891.

It was an instant success. The class period ended with a 1–0 score, with the only goal scored by William Chase, and word of the new game soon spread. In the next few weeks, the game began to draw spectators. Part of the game's appeal was the fact that it was easy to learn and could be played by people with a wide range of abilities. It even caught the interest of female teachers at the nearby Buckingham School, who organized the first women's basketball team and played in the gym. The spectators also helped to bring changes to the game. With so many people in the gallery, it was easy for someone to deflect the ball away from the basket, so Naismith added a board behind the basket. This prevented fan interference, but it also had the unintentional effect of making it easier to score, and the innovation has remained long after the baskets were moved away from spectator areas.

Despite the game's popularity, Naismith himself only played in two games in his lifetime, one of which was on March 11, 1892. Less than three months after he invented the game, the gymnasium's gallery was filled with over two hundred spectators who came to watch a game between the faculty and students. Referred to in the *Springfield Republican* headline as a "Basket Football Game," it is generally considered to have been the first public basketball game, and Naismith played on the faculty team along with Gulick, Stagg and four other teachers. The faculty lost 5–1, with Stagg scoring their only basket. He was dressed in his Yale football uniform, and the *Republican* remarked that "his football training hampered him, and he was perpetually making fouls and shoving his opponents." The students, who presumably benefitted from more practice

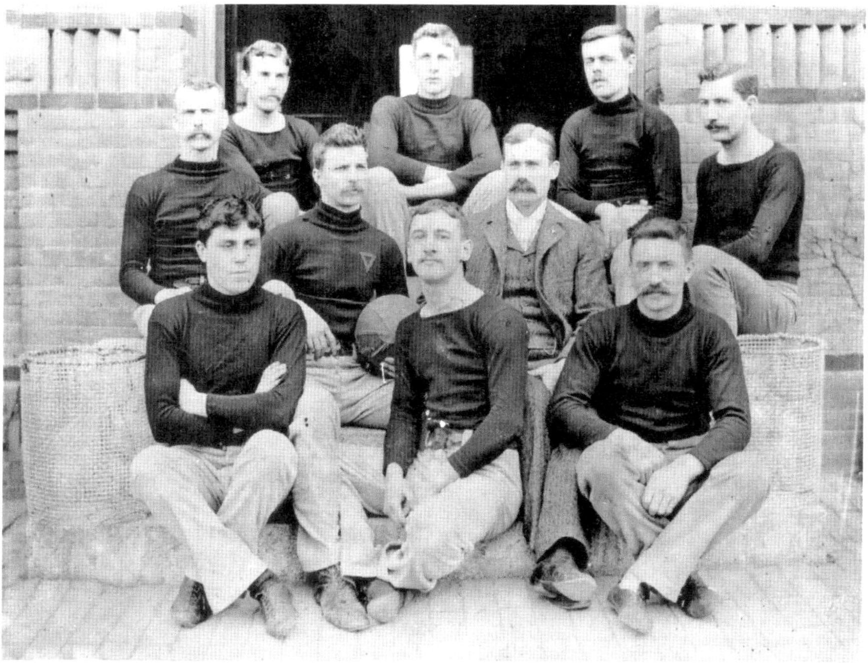

James Naismith in 1892 with nine players from the first basketball game, including William Chase (*back row, right*) who scored the game's only point. *Springfield College, Babson Library, Archives and Special Collections.*

than the teachers, were led by Edwin Ruggles, who "tossed the ball into the illusive basket four times." Despite the lopsided score, though, the newspaper reported that "the spectators followed the game with much interest and amusement."

Basketball's popularity soon spread beyond Springfield, aided in part by the YMCA, who introduced the game in its locations across the country. Naismith himself remained in Springfield for just a few more years. In 1894, he married Springfield native Maude Sherman, and the next year, they moved to Denver, where he had been offered a job at a YMCA facility. While in Denver, he earned his medical degree, and in 1898, he took a job teaching and coaching basketball at the University of Kansas. Naismith remained there for almost forty years, eventually serving as the school's athletic director, and he lived to see basketball become an Olympic sport for the first time in the 1936 Summer Olympics. Naismith died three years later, but his legacy is remembered both in Kansas, where the basketball teams play on the James Naismith Court, and here in Springfield, with the Naismith Memorial Basketball Hall of Fame.

As for the building where he first invented the game, the YMCA Training School only remained for several more years. The school had purchased property along the Watershops Pond in 1891, and over the next few years, the organization began building a new campus. By 1896, the YMCA school had completely moved out of the School for Christian Workers building at Winchester Square, and it has remained at the new location ever since. The school was renamed Springfield College in 1954, and although it offers degrees in a wide range of studies, it still has a strong emphasis on physical education–related fields.

The original building was located at the corner of State and Sherman Streets, but by the 1890s, it was expanded to cover the entire width of the block between Sherman and Catherine Streets. The School for Christian Workers, which was later renamed the Bible Normal College, left the building soon after the training school, relocating to Hartford in 1897. By 1910, the building was known as Winchester Chambers, a rooming house that offered single-room units and suites for residents, with stores on the first floor.

It remained a rooming house until 1961, at which point fewer than 40 of the building's 140 units were occupied, and the owner wanted to redevelop the site with a shopping plaza. The building was heavily damaged in a fire in December, and it was demolished soon after to build a parking lot for the shopping plaza. In 1995, a McDonald's restaurant was built on the

Sherman Street side of the parking lot, on the spot where the original section of the School for Christian Workers building, including the gymnasium, had once stood.

# BIBLIOGRAPHY

*Acts and Resolves Passed by the General Court of Massachusetts in the Year 1913*. Boston: Wright & Potter Printing Co., 1913.

Adams, William Frederick. *Everett Hosmer Barney: His Family Connections, A Record of His Life Work. George Murray Barney*. Springfield, MA: Privately printed, 1912.

*American Biography: A New Cyclopedia.* Vol. 2. New York: American Historical Society, 1918.

*Atlas of the City of Springfield Massachusetts*. Springfield, MA: L.J. Richards & Co., 1899.

Barrows, Charles Henry. *The Poets and Poetry of Springfield in Massachusetts, From Early Times to the End of the Nineteenth Century*. Springfield, MA: Connecticut Valley Historical Society, 1907.

Bates, William G. *An Address, Delivered in the New Court House, in Springfield, Hampden County, Massachusetts*. Springfield, MA: Clark W. Bryan & Company, 1874.

Bauer, Frank. *At the Crossroads: Springfield, Massachusetts 1636–1975*. Springfield, MA: U.S.A. Bicentennial Committee of Springfield, 1975.

*Biographical Review. This Volume Contains Biographical Sketches of the Leading Citizens of Hampden County, Massachusetts.* Boston: Biographical Review Publishing Company, 1895.

Bishop, J. Leander. *A History of American Manufactures from 1608 to 1860.* Vol. 2. Philadelphia: Edward Young & Co., 1864.

Boudreau, Robert. "Springfield Union Station." *Passenger Train Journal* 124 (April 1988): 24–30.

Buckingham, James Silk. *The Eastern and Western States of America.* London: Fisher, Son & Co., 1842.

Burt, Henry M. *The First Century of the History of Springfield: The Official Records from 1636 to 1736, with an Historical Review and Biographical Mention of the Founders.* Springfield, MA: Henry M. Burt, 1898.

Chapin, Charles Wells. *Sketches of the Old Inhabitants and Other Citizens of Old Springfield of the Present Century and Its Historic Mansions of "Ye Olden Tyme."* Springfield, MA: Springfield Printing and Binding Company, 1893.

Chicoine, David R. *Guns of the New West: A Close-Up Look at Modern Replica Firearms.* Iola, WI: Gun Digest Books, 2005.

Clapp, Ebenezer. *The Clapp Memorial.* Boston: David Clapp & Son, 1876.

Cohen, Charles D. *The Seuss, the Whole Seuss, and Nothing but the Seuss: A Visual Biography of Theodor Seuss Geisel.* New York: Random House, 2004.

Connecticut Valley Historical Society. *Springfield, Massachusetts: A Maintenance Fund of One Hundred Thousand Dollars to Be Established by Members and Friends of the Society.* Springfield: Connecticut Valley Historical Society, 1912.

Copeland, Alfred Minot. *"Our County and Its People" A History of Hampden County Massachusetts.* Boston: Century Memorial Publishing Company, 1902.

Crackel, Theodore J. "Revolutionary War Pension Records and Patterns of American Mobility, 1780–1830." *Prologue Magazine*, Fall 1984.

D'Amato, Donald J. *Springfield—350 Years: A Pictorial History*. Norfolk, VA: Donning Company/Publishers, 1985.

Du Bois, W.E.B. *John Brown*. Philadelphia: George W. Jacobs & Company, 1909.

Dwight, Benjamin Woodbridge. *The History of the Descendants of John Dwight, of Dedham, Mass*. New York: John F. Trow & Son, 1874.

Dzierzak, Lou. *The Evolution of American Bicycle Racing*. Guilford, CT: Falcon Guides, 2007.

Earle, Alice Morse. *Stage-Coach and Tavern Days*. New York: Macmillan Company, 1902.

Elliott, Cecil D. *The American Architect from the Colonial Era to the Present*. Jefferson, NC: McFarland & Company, 2003.

*The First Church: Springfield, Massachusetts 1637–1915; Milestones Through Twenty-Seven Decades*. Springfield, MA: F.A. Bassette Co., 1915.

Frisch, Michael H. *Town into City: Springfield, Massachusetts, and the Meaning of Community, 1840–1880*. Cambridge, MA: Harvard University Press, 1972.

Gardner, Eugene C. *Springfield Present and Prospective*. Springfield, MA: Pond & Campbell, 1905.

Glasson, William Henry. *History of Military Pension Legislation in the United States*. New York: Columbia University Press, 1900.

Goldberg, Vicki. *Lewis W. Hine: Children at Work*. Munich: Prestel, 1999.

Green, Mason A. *Springfield, 1636–1886: History of Town and City; Including an Account of the Quarter Millennial Celebration at Springfield, Mass., May 25 and 26, 1886*. Springfield, MA: C.A. Nichols, 1888.

Hearn, Daniel Allen. *Legal Executions in New England: A Comprehensive Reference, 1623–1960*. Jefferson, NC: McFarland & Company, 1999.

Hitchcock, Henry-Russell. *The Architecture of H.H. Richardson and His Times*. Cambridge, MA: MIT Press, 1970.

———. *Springfield Architecture 1800–1900*. Springfield, MA: Springfield City Library, 1980.

Jenkins, Stephen. *The Old Boston Post Road*. New York: Knickerbocker Press, 1913.

Jinks, Roy G., and Sandra C. Krein. *Smith & Wesson*. Charleston, SC: Arcadia Publishing, 2006.

King, Moses. *King's Handbook of Springfield, Massachusetts: A Series of Monographs, Historical and Descriptive*. Springfield, MA: J.D. Gill, 1884.

Konig, Michael F., and Martin Kaufman. *Springfield, 1636–1986*. Springfield, MA: Springfield Library and Museums Association, 1987.

MacKenzie, Alex. *Springfield Armory*. Charleston, SC: Arcadia Publishing, 2015.

Miller, Glenn T. *Piety and Profession: American Protestant Theological Education, 1870–1970*. Grand Rapids, MI: William B. Eerdmans Publishing, 2007.

Morris, Edmund. *The Rise of Theodore Roosevelt*. New York: Modern Library, 1979.

Morris, Henry. *History of the First Church in Springfield*. Springfield, MA: Whitney & Adams, 1875.

*The National Cyclopedia of American Biography*. Vol. 10. New York: James T. White & Company, 1900.

Nelson, David M. *The Anatomy of a Game: Football, the Rules, and the Men Who Made the Game*. Newark: University of Delaware Press, 1994.

Oates, Stephen B. *To Purge This Land with Blood: A Biography of John Brown*. Amherst: University of Massachusetts Press, 1984.

Okrent, Daniel. *Last Call: The Rise and Fall of Prohibition*. New York: Scribner, 2010.

Parsons, Henry. *Parsons Family: Descendants of Cornet Joseph Parsons Springfield, 1636—Northampton, 1655*. New York: Frank Allaben Genealogical Company, 1912.

Plunkett, Harriette Merrick Hodge. *Josiah Gilbert Holland*. New York: Charles Scribner's Sons, 1894.

Powell, S.W. "Progressive Methods of Church Work." *Christian Union*. February 6, 1892.

Professional Football Researchers Association. "Camp and His Followers." http://www.profootballresearchers.org/articles/Camp_And_Followers.pdf.

Raber, Michael S., et al. *Conservative Innovators and Military Small Arms: An Industrial History of the Springfield Armory, 1794–1968*. South Glastonbury, CT: Raber Associates, 1989.

Rains, Rob, and Hellen Carpenter. *James Naismith: The Man Who Invented Basketball*. Philadelphia: Temple University Press, 2009.

Reynolds, David S. *John Brown, Abolitionist*. New York: Alfred A. Knopf, 2005.

Richey, Albert S. *Traffic and Operation: Springfield Street Railway Company, Springfield, Massachusetts*. N.p: 1917.

Rogers, Alan. *Murder and the Death Penalty in Massachusetts*. Amherst: University of Massachusetts Press, 2008.

*Rules and Regulations of the Public Schools of the City of Springfield*. Springfield, MA: Samuel Bowles and Company, 1867.

Sapp, Rick. *Revolvers*. Charlotte, NC: TAJ Books International, 2014.

Smith, Andrew F. *Food and Drink in American History*. Vol. 1. Santa Barbara, CA: ABC-CLIO, 2013.

*Springfield Homestead*. "Passing of the Old Tavern: Uncle Jeremy Warriner's Old Coffee House—Where He Entertained Such Notables as Kossuth and Jenny Lind." February 6, 1907.

St. John, Allen, and Ainissa G. Ramirez. *Newton's Football: The Science Behind America's Game*. New York: Ballantine Books, 2013.

U.S. Census Bureau. *Census of Population and Housing*. http://www.census.gov/prod/www/decennial.html.

———. "Fourteenth Census of the United States." 1920. https://familysearch.org/search/collection/1488411.

———. "Thirteenth Census of the United States." 1910. *FamilySearch*. https://familysearch.org/search/collection/1727033.

———. "Twelfth Census of the United States." 1900. *FamilySearch*. https://familysearch.org/search/collection/1325221.

U.S. Congress. *The Debates and Proceedings in the Congress of the United States*. 8th Cong., 1st sess. Washington, D.C.: Gales and Seaton, 1852.

Vose, George L. *Notes on Early Transportation in Massachusetts: A Paper Read before the Boston Society of Civil Engineers, November 18, 1884*. New York: Atkin & Prout, 1884.

Whittlesey, Derwent Stainthorpe. "The Springfield Armory: A Study in Institutional Development." PhD diss., University of Chicago, 1920.

Wight, Charles Albert. *Some Old Time Meeting Houses of the Connecticut Valley*. Chicopee Falls, MA: Rich Print, 1911.

## NEWSPAPERS

*Boston Globe*
*Chicago Tribune*
*Springfield Homestead*
*Springfield Republican*
*Springfield Union*

## WEBSITES

baseball-reference.com
founders.archives.gov
masslive.com
mhc-macris.net
newsbank.com
profootballresearchers.org

# INDEX

# ABOUT THE AUTHOR

Derek Strahan is a Springfield resident and the author of the blog *Lost New England*. He is a graduate of Westfield State University with degrees in English and regional planning, and he teaches English at The Master's School in Simsbury, Connecticut.

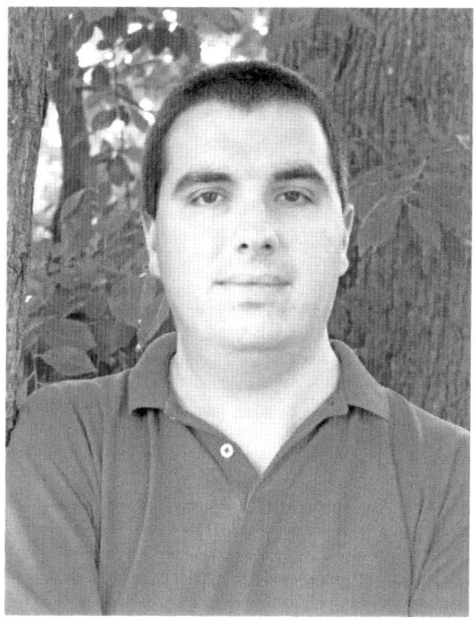